RAF
MANSTON
ALBUM

R.A.F. MANSTON HISTORY CLUB

SUTTON PUBLISHING

RAF Manston was first published in 1993 by
Sutton Publishing Limited

RAF Manston A Second Selection was first published in 1994 by
Sutton Publishing Limited

This combined edition first published in 2001 by
Sutton Publishing Limited · Phoenix mill
Thrupp · Stroud · Gloucestershire · GL5 2BU

Reprinted 2005

Copyright © RAF Manston History Club, 1993, 1994, 2001

ISBN 0 7509 2913 8

Typesetting and origination by
Sutton Publishing Limited
Printed and bound in Great Britain by
J.H. Haynes & Co. Ltd, Sparkford.

RAF
MANSTON
ALBUM

PART ONE

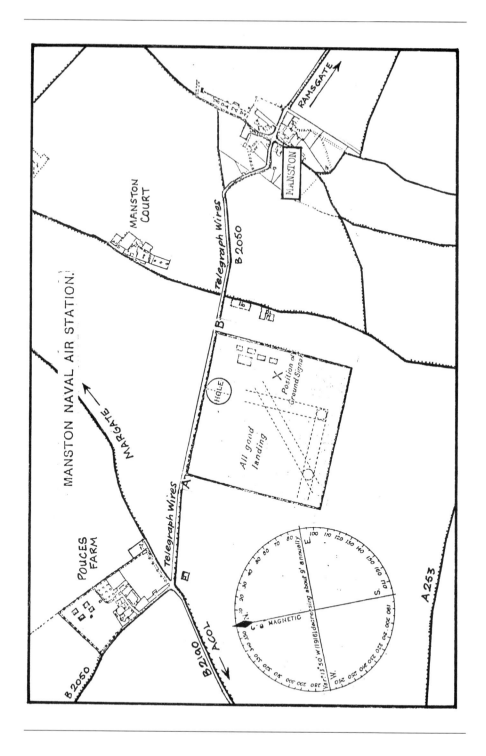

Contents

Foreword

When I was first asked to write a foreword to this intriguing book I knew that I could not decline so flattering an invitation and I began to consider what I should say about it. My thoughts centred on the word 'history': what does it mean and include? I looked in several dictionaries, all of which gave a number of different definitions, and the one which I decided best describes both the intent and content of this work was: 'All that is preserved or remembered of people, places and events in the past, especially in written or pictorial form.' The RAF Manston History Club has many rememberers and a good selection of preservers and they have combined and cooperated to produce, 'in written or pictorial form', a fascinating cross-section of the station's history.

RAF Manston's story is only a few years shorter than that of military aviation and reflects in many ways the developments that have taken place over the years. Its unorthodox buildings pre-date the more typical red-brick design of those that were built in the 1930s, giving it a unique character.

Seventy-seven years is not long in historical context but in that time Manston has performed a variety of functions unsurpassed by any other British aerodrome, as these pages will testify.

I was fortunate enough to serve as Station Intelligence Officer from 8 August 1940 until March 1943 and I think that covered the most exciting period in the station's history. The aerodrome's situation so close to the coast of mainland Europe (France is plainly visible on a clear day) meant that it was not only the most frequently attacked British airfield but that it was used, as the war progressed, as a take-off point for all sorts of offensive operations. Aircraft of every type and of every Command (and even the Navy) made use of Manston as an emergency landing ground or as a temporary or semi-permanent base, and the requirements of their pilots and crews and their machines were the responsibility of the station personnel.

Manston's reputation as a place where everything was happening made it a popular venue for VIPs: we were visited by Winston Churchill, de Gaulle, Montgomery, Trenchard and a host of others. Dull moments were rare in those days. Looking back, I regret that I did not keep a personal diary and that I did not take more photographs. I did produce a daily intelligence bulletin which I know was continued after I left and a copy of each issue was duly stored away, but I never heard what became of them.

But the two-and-a-half years of which I can speak represent only about 4 per cent of the station's life and a great deal has happened in the other 96 per cent, as the following pages will show. Although I served on a number of other stations and headquarters during the later part of the war, none has the same appeal for me. I am sure that I am not alone in regarding it with genuine affection. Why else would the producers of this book have spent so much time and effort in collecting and collating all the material? They did it because, like me, they love RAF Manston. Long may its history continue!

H. Smith

Introduction

No history of Manston may be considered complete without first noting its relationship to the nearby Westgate-on-Sea base, established in July 1914 by the Royal Naval Air Service (RNAS) as a seaplane station for Thames Estuary patrols in response to the threat of war with Germany.

In January 1915 a small aerodrome was also opened on the adjacent clifftop, where the sunken garden is now located, for operations by landplanes against raiding airships and aircraft. Flying from such a restricted area, especially at night, proved to be unacceptably hazardous and in the winter of 1915–16 the Commanding Officer of Westgate, Sq. Cdr. R.P. Ross, persuaded the Admiralty that a larger aerodrome was essential. As a result 20 acres of Manston Court Farm were taken over in early 1916, initially as a night-landing ground only, and the first recorded operational use was made by Fl. Lt. H.A. Buss who landed there (having taken off from Westgate) on the night of 19 March 1916 in the course of an abortive sortie against a non-existent airship. Manston was officially regarded as fully operational from 25 May 1916, by which date the pilots, aircraft and attendant personnel had moved in from Westgate. From June this small flying unit was known as the War Flight, tasked with carrying out inshore patrols and the air defence of the area against German air raids. On 9 July it flew its first operation from the new base, and this was the first of more than 140 sorties it mounted in the following year and a half – in spite of an average strength of only six pilots and never more than ten. The summer of 1916 brought a lodger unit to Manston temporarily in the form of No. 3 Wing, RNAS, engaged in working up in preparation for a move to eastern France to carry out the world's first strategic bombing campaign against industrial targets on the Rhine. The Wing eventually departed in October.

Plans were also in hand for the creation of heavy bomber squadrons equipped with the new large twin-engined Handley Page aircraft just becoming available. A training school for these air and ground crews was formed at Manston in September 1916, and it continued to operate there until moving to Stonehenge in January 1918. The naval flying school at Eastchurch was transferred to Manston during the spring of 1917 and was re-titled the War School. The autumn of the year marked the establishment of the Southern Training Base for the large number of mechanics then being recruited.

Considerable construction work was undertaken from early in the year, comprising both technical and domestic building. Among the former were semi-underground (or sunken) hangars, two of the projected five being virtually completed by the end of the First World War.

The demand for pilots on the Western Front at this time necessitated enlargement of, and some changes in, the function of the War School, which became the Pilots' Pool in March/April 1918. With the formation of the RAF on 1 April this unit was renamed 203 Training Depot Station (TDS) with a normal strength the equivalent of three two-seater squadrons. Having rendered distinguished service in the Home Defence role since mid-1916 the War Flight was now relieved of this duty, and became the landplane element of the newly formed No. 219 Squadron whose primary function was escorting the Westgate seaplanes of that unit patrolling off the Kent Coast. In July 203 TDS was renumbered 55 TDS, and moved to Narborough, Norfolk, in September. Manston was now at its peak strength in the First World War and a complex of huts had been erected to house the 2,500 personnel: the aerodrome and camp area exceeded 650 acres. A new unit, No. 2 Observer's School, was formed in September and operated until a year later, when No. 1 (Observers) School of Aerial Gunnery from New Romney replaced it.

Yet another removal was that of the Pilots' Pool to Joyce Green, Dartford, in October. The main remaining flying activities by then consisted of patrols by No. 219 Squadron in search of wartime sea-mines adrift in the Thames Estuary and adjacent waters, a task it fulfilled until disbanded in February 1920.

The growth of Manston and its anticipated continued use later in the war called for improved facilities for the transport of heavy goods to and from the camp, and in 1919 a single track, standard gauge rail link was laid to join the main Ramsgate–London line at Birchington.

Peace in 1918 brought great changes and development to Manston. The School of Technical Training moved in from Halton, followed by No. 6 Flying Training School using Avro 504s, Bristol Fighters and Sopwith Snipes among others. New roads were built through the camp with its, by now numerous, buildings of all kinds.

The 'Geddes Axe' fell in 1922, with pay cuts for the Services and consequent reductions in the School of Technical Training, while the FTS was disbanded. No. 2 Army Cooperation Squadron came to Manston in 1924 followed by the reformed No. 3 Squadron – thus bringing back the Snipes and Bristol Fighters. Some of these arrived by train from Birchington using the spur, mentioned earlier, which terminated in the very centre of the camp. Later No. 3 Squadron's planes were replaced by the Vickers Virginias of No. 9 Squadron.

1926 saw Manston transferred from 1 Group to 23 Group, and about this time 135 officers and men were sent away to defend Kidbrooke stores depot during the General Strike. No. 2 Squadron left for Shanghai in 1927, later to return and lose two aircraft in accidents, one having a collision with a No. 9 Squadron Virginia. During this period Oxford University Air Squadron spent its summer camp at Manston as also did No. 600 Squadron, both participating in the Air Defence of Great Britain exercises of that year.

The Bristol Fighters of No. 2 Squadron were replaced by Armstrong Whitworth Atlas aircraft in 1930, and that October Manston provided a guard of honour when the fatalities from the R101 airship crash were brought home via Dover.

In March 1931 No. 500 Squadron (County of Kent) was formed, equipped with Virginias, the first being christened *Isle of Thanet*. Later in the year No. 9 Squadron moved to Boscombe Down, having spent six years in Thanet.

Yet another transfer in 1932, from 23 to 22 Group, saw Nos 821 and 822 Squadrons, FAA, at Manston with their Fairey 111Fs, having disembarked from HMS *Courageous* and HMS *Furious*. During the next few years a regular air service was inaugurated between Thanet and London, while in 1934 6,000 people attended the first Empire Air Day at the airfield. No. 2 Squadron was replaced in 1935 by No. 48 Squadron, equipped with Avro Ansons and Saro Cloud amphibians. More Ansons came in later with the School of Air Navigation. The station then transferred into No. 24 (Training) Group and No. 206 Squadron reformed, also with Ansons. Two high-speed launches were based at Ramsgate for duty with No. 48 (General Reconnaisaance) Squadron and the Virginias of No. 500 Squadron were replaced by Hawker Hart light bombers. The School of Air Navigation now became responsible for its own flying with the Ansons, and No. 48 Squadron moved away to Eastchurch to become operational.

1938 found No. 500 Squadron, now on Hawker Hinds, moving to Detling, as Manston concentrated on the build-up of personnel and equipment following the Munich crisis. Anti-aircraft gunposts were set up and the bomb dump was established, while buildings and aircraft took on the camouflage colours that were to remain throughout the coming conflict.

Located on the Thanet coastline, Manston became part of the RAF's 'cutting edge' in the battles with the Luftwaffe during Germany's attempts to subjugate Fighter Command and control the skies of Southern England in the darkest days of the Second World War. As a forward airfield during the Battle of Britain the station suffered numerous attacks by bomb, cannon and machine-gun, being only 10 minutes' flying time from Luftwaffe bases in France.

The airfield played host to many famous squadrons of No. 11 Group, Fighter Command, under whose control it operated from November 1939. The early months of the Battle of Britain saw Luftwaffe pressure concentrated on the RAF with attacks on the forward airfields and RDF (Radio Direction Finding – the original name for radar) stations along the Channel coast. Manston bore the brunt of these raids, which in August alone amounted to seven consecutive attacks – in one of which over a hundred bombs were dropped, resulting in a much cratered airfield.

Air and ground crews suffered heavy casualties under the incessant onslaught, and at one stage all administrative and non-essential personnel were evacuated and dispersed to various locations throughout the Thanet area. The Battle of Britain drew to a close and by November 1940 the Luftwaffe's assault on airfields and radar stations had been defeated by the gallant 'few' of

RAF Fighter Command. Their triumph changed the face of history and set this country on the road to ultimate victory. It was from Manston that so many of these brave pilots flew their Hurricanes, Spitfires, Blenheims and Defiants, invariably against overwhelming odds, continuing the fight despite the heavy losses they sustained.

After the intense activities of 1940 Manston prepared to take the fight to the enemy, and a veritable parade of RAF squadrons operated from there through the rest of the war on a variety of duties. These units took on the Luftwaffe on its home ground, and over the next three years Manston became the springboard for mounting attacks against a well-armed and entrenched enemy. One such operation, led by Lt. Cdr. Esmonde, against German naval units in the Channel, became a byword for courage in the face of murderous defensive fire. Taking-off from Manston on 12 February 1942, Esmonde led six Swordfish biplane torpedo-bombers of No. 825 Squadron, FAA, into the attack. Such was the ferocity of the defences of the *Scharnhorst, Gneisenau, Prinz Eugen* and their escort ships that none of the slow and poorly armed Swordfish returned. For this action Esmonde was awarded a posthumous Victoria Cross.

In August 1942 the Allies attempted a landing at Dieppe – Operation Jubilee – which began with a concentrated air assault, the squadrons from Manston taking a full and active part. After a titanic struggle to overcome the German defences the order was given to withdraw. The lessons learned at Dieppe helped the Allies to prepare for the Second Front and particularly D-Day.

The mighty Typhoon and sleek Whirlwind fighters continued their low-level operations against enemy targets across the Channel, keeping up the pressure on a now somewhat hard-pressed Luftwaffe. While these offensive operations were in progress the construction of a 3,000 yd long runway was begun. This was to prove a Godsend to Allied aircraft and crews damaged in the fierce combats over Europe. Its value was further enhanced by the introduction of FIDO, a device to disperse fog. It consisted of pipes along the runway sides from which petrol was pumped and ignited, thereby 'lifting' the fog and enabling pilots to locate the runway and land when limited visibility prevailed.

With the invasion of 'Fortress Europe' on 6 June 1944 aircraft from Manston helped pave the way for the ground forces by repeated attacks on troop concentrations, bridges, railways and armour. Shortly after D-Day Hitler unleashed his V1 weapon – the flying bomb. To combat this new threat the RAF's latest fighter aircraft, including the jet-powered Gloster Meteor and powerful Hawker Tempest, operated from Manston, which by then found itself almost beneath the flight path of these doodle-bugs when en route to London across Kent. Thanks to the efforts of our pilots many of the flying bombs were destroyed before reaching their targets.

Many squadrons of the Allied air forces flew from this airfield throughout the Second World War and pilots and aircrew from nearly every corner of the globe took part in sorties against the enemy – South Africans, Rhodesians, New Zealanders, Free French and Belgians, Canadians, Americans, British, Polish, Czechs and Norwegians. The station also afforded a safe haven to the crews of Bomber Command and the USAF returning with crippled aircraft and wounded crew members after raids on the Reich, although many failed to reach Manston and crashed or forcelanded in Thanet.

This, then, was the story of Manston during the Second World War, one of hardship and valour. The station was a shield when Britain stood alone, but became a launch-pad to victory. The courage and determination of the Service and civilian personnel maintained the vital functions on the station. The bravery so often exhibited is epitomized by the actions of Fire Officer Twyman and Fireman Watson of the Margate Fire Brigade, who were awarded the George Medal for their heroic efforts during a heavy raid on the airfield.

With the coming of the Cold War across Europe the Western Powers began to step up their defences and adopt a more united posture. The US Strategic Air Command (SAC) decided to use Manston as a rotational base for their units employed in the fighter-bomber role. It was, indeed, the first RAF station in the United Kingdom to be so used by SAC in the post-Second World War period. Each unit served ninety days on temporary duty and the station's facilities were shared by the RAF and USAF. On 11 July 1950 the 7512th Air Base Squadron was established at Manston, tasked to provide support and administration services for the intended resident wings and squadrons. The first of these arrived in July 1950, comprising the 20th Fighter-Bomber Wing and elements of that group.

1951 saw the arrival of the 31st and 12th Fighter-Escort Wings and, in December, the 123rd Fighter-Bomber Wing, this last being a National Air Guard unit. When the 123rd FB Wing returned to the USA in July 1952 some personnel and equipment remained to become part of the 406th Fighter-Bomber Wing, destined to stay at Manston until May 1958. Another long-time resident unit was the 92nd Fighter-Bomber Squadron, from March 1955 to April 1958. When the 406th was inactivated, its personnel and equipment were transferred to other SAC units. Among the units at Manston in the years of American occupation were those providing air sea rescue facilities in the seas around south-east England. For this task they flew Albatross amphibian and S-55 helicopters, the forerunners of similar search and rescue services provided in following years by the RAF and civil operators. The end of the American period came in June 1958 when Manston was handed back to the RAF.

The story of civil aviation and airline operations at Manston is largely that of the entrepreneurial Wing Commander Hugh C. Kennard DFC, RAF (Retd) who, from 1959 onwards, initiated, operated, owned or participated in numerous companies operating from Manston, which by then was available to both RAF and civil authorities. The first airline operations were those of Silver City Airways who, in 1959, commenced passenger charter flights and troop carrying on a world-wide basis, using Handley Page Hermes and Douglas Dakota aircraft. In the following years such companies as Invicta Airways, Air Ferry, Air Holdings and Interland Air Services were the operators at various times, engaged in the transportation of passengers, freight and cars. The result of these activities was the rebuilding of the airport terminal on more than one occasion and the establishment of adequate maintenance facilities for the business, generated not only by the companies resident at Manston but from elsewhere in the UK and abroad. This continues to be the situation today.

This book does not attempt to bring events up to the present at Manston, but ends in the mid-1960s, when recovery from the Second World War had hardly begun. Many other units and activities have joined the Manston story since then, and we apologize to those who have not been mentioned. In the future we hope that the story of this famous airfield will be continued in book form with the omissions rectified.

SECTION ONE

In the Beginning : 1916–1919

The earliest intimation of Westgate's future role as a seaplane base in the First World War came with the arrival of three machines to participate in fleet exercises in June 1914. Based in St Mildred's Bay, their presence and activities from the 15th to the 18th aroused great interest among the townspeople and holiday visitors, as this photograph demonstrates.

This tranquil scene on the sands of St Mildred's Bay gives no hint of the war-like purpose to which the area would be put very shortly, with the establishment of the RNAS seaplane base for patrols over the estuary of the Thames. Taken in August 1914, the presence of the military airship, *Astra Torres*, on patrol indicates the onset of the First World War.

On 29 July RNAS personnel arrived to staff Westgate, which the Admiralty decided to open as a permanent base for escort and patrol duties as a result of the satisfactory reports from the station. Flt. Cdr. J.T. Babington, the first Commanding Officer, arrived in Short seaplane No. 120 on 2 August, two days before war with Germany was declared. The handling crew are shown launching this machine at about this time.

A typical scene on the cliff-top aerodrome at Westgate, 1915. An air raid warning has been made and the BE.2c and its crew are about to depart. The officer with the telescope is reputed to be the CO, Sqn. Cdr. Ross, who obviously believed in personal supervision when his other duties permitted. The BE type was one of a variety of aeroplanes in use at Westgate for defence against the German air raids.

Sqn. Cdr. Robert Peel Ross, who assumed command of Westgate in September 1915 and of Manston. The establishment of Manston, in fact, can be wholly attributed to Ross, whose overtures to the Admiralty for a safer aerodrome than initially existed at Westgate finally prevailed. For many months he was the CO of both Westgate and Manston. After a distinguished RAF career Ross retired as an air commodore in 1934.

From the beginning the RNAS Westgate personnel enjoyed the full cooperation of the local people. Prominent among these were Sir William Ingram, proprietor of the *Illustrated London News*, and his son Bertie. Accommodation for the officers was made available by Sir William in St Mildred's Hotel, which he owned, until quarters became available. Some of these fortunate guests are shown about to depart from the hotel's elaborate entrance.

A line-up of some of the Westgate aeroplanes, 1915. From the left, an Avro, a Bristol Scout and a BE.2c. This view to the east clearly shows the houses in Westonville Avenue. The aerodrome, half a mile long and a quarter of a mile wide, was created by requisitioning the land from its owners, the Bethlem Hospital and William Hedgcock, who farmed the area along the clifftop.

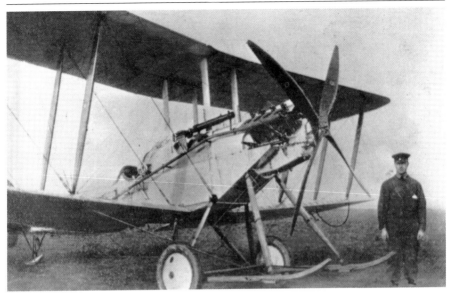

Pictured here is BE.2c aircraft 1159, one of the landplanes flown at Westgate from November 1915 to March 1916. Its most significant flight was probably on the night of 19/20 March 1916, when it made the first recorded use of Manston following an anti-Zeppelin sortie by Flt. Lt. H.A. Buss. The Lewis machine-gun, being unsynchronized, might well damage or destroy the propeller blades – another hazard of early warplanes.

This Bristol Scout, 8951, seen at Westgate in May or June 1916, made a number of defence sorties from there and subsequently from Manston where it served in the War Flight until May 1917. Its pilot on most occasions was a New Zealander, Flt. Lt. J.H. Carr, one of the many officers from all parts of the Empire who served at Westgate and Manston. The single Lewis machine-gun is mounted above the top wing.

The primary function of Westgate was in the sphere of seaplane operations – providing escorts for the shipping in the Thames mouth and the offshore waters of the Kent coast, with particular attention to enemy submarine activities. This Short 827 seaplane is being prepared for just such an operation in 1916. The location is the concrete hardstanding in front of the main hangar.

A view across the seaplane base, August 1917. In the distance is the signal station and to the right the large hangar, 200 ft long, which was erected, along with a heavy wooden ramp to the sands, in the latter part of 1915. The presence of bell tents implies that the accelerated expansion of the base brought accommodation difficulties. Fortunately this occurred in the summer months.

Launching seaplanes or flying boats was always a tricky, tedious and labour-intensive task especially in high winds and rough seas. The answer to the difficulty at Westgate was the use of this launching trolley, which ran down timbers laid on the sand. Here Short 827 is approaching the water, complete with trolley, under its own power. The handling party are wearing armpit-length waders.

The main hangar, the parking areas for the seaplanes, and the wooden launching/landing ramp mentioned earlier, 1918. The aperture below the seaplane marked '5' was the pre-First World War launching ramp for small boats and yachts. This was covered with timber decking so as to enlarge the parking area available for seaplanes.

The final layout of Westgate, 1918. The compact nature of the base, despite its constant war activities, many seaplanes and large number of personnel, is noteworthy and in contrast to the customary widespread character of the average air station. The two hangars, with various ancillary buildings, are in the centre. The white structures, bottom right, are brick barrack blocks. The officers' mess is centre left with Beach Road and Old Boundary Road at either end of that block.

One of the earliest photographs of Manston aerodrome, thought to have been taken in May or June 1916. One wooden hangar and another of canvas housed the aircraft, with the personnel occupying the huts seen at the right. The work of erecting the first buildings at Manston was carried out by naval ratings who travelled over daily from Westgate.

BE.2c No. 8298, of the War Flight, Manston, which had a particularly long and active service against the German raiders. It was a favourite mount of Sqn. Cdr. C.H. Butler who, as the War Flight's CO, made many sorties with 8298 between mid-1916 and early 1918. This photograph is interesting, also, in that it shows the hangar transferred to Manston from Westgate when that aerodrome was closed.

For a considerable time after the opening of Manston it continued to come under the control of Westgate and shared the same CO, Sqn. Cdr. Ross. The operational unit was a small one, known as the War Flight. Flying crews continued to live at Westgate and travelled to and from Manston as their duties required. This Lancia was one of the vehicles used. The driver on this occasion was Air Mechanic Cornwall.

The first air-to-ground view of Manston, 1916. It provides a complete picture of the new aerodrome, little more than a quarter of a mile square. The photograph was taken from above Manston village and looks westward. Hangars and living accommodation already exist (foreground) with preliminary development near Pouces Farm in progress.

Above Pouces Farm and looking east, 1916. The cross-road at centre bottom was then, as it remains, a dominant feature of what was to become the Main Camp at Manston. The road that crosses the aerodrome now (but did not do so in 1916) shows up prominently, leading to Manston village at the top of the picture. The black vertical marks on this print are bracing wires on the photographing aeroplane.

The welfare of the personnel at Manston was not overlooked by the citizens and organizations of the towns in Thanet. Here, a recreation hut presented by the Church of England Temperance Society is opened by Alderman Chayney and his wife in July, 1916. The occasion was attended by a number of dignitaries from the district and even more from the Royal Navy and Army.

In May 1916 a 'lodger unit' in the form of No. 3 Wing, RNAS, moved into Manston for a working-up period before undertaking the task of bombing industrial targets in the Saar. This was the first strategic bombing campaign attempted by an air force. In October the Wing had moved to eastern France where it was to be based. Sopwith 1½ Strutter aeroplanes of No. 3 Wing are shown while at Manston.

Rose Cottage in the snow of December 1916. During the First World War it was the living quarters of officers pending the construction of permanent camp buildings. It is now named Holmcroft, and is the residence of the commanding officers of Manston.

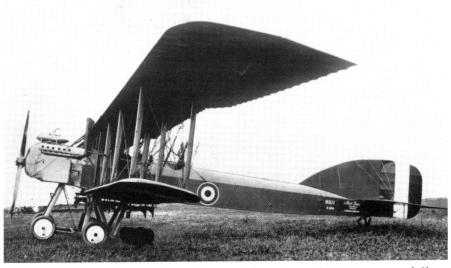

During its stay at Manston No. 3 Wing had both Sopwith 1½ Strutter and Short bombers, one of which is illustrated. This particular machine, 9311, was on the Wing's strength for only a few days before being presented to the French. The type was not popular with the flying crews who were, no doubt, relieved when the decision was taken to equip the Wing wholly with Sopwith aeroplanes.

The formation of Handley Page-equipped bombing squadrons necessitated new and special training facilities for the crews so the Handley Page Training Squadron was created at Manston in December 1916. Four pupils, Flight Sub-Lieutenants Allen, Andrews, Johnson and Young, are shown before their billet in the winter of 1916–17.

Late 1916 saw the introduction of these large, twin-engined bombers, the Handley Page 0/100. Some of the earliest were destined for No. 3 Wing and were to be flown to eastern France. Unfortunately this one, No. 1463 (*La Amazone*), became lost in bad weather en route from Manston, and was captured by German troops after landing near Laon. No. 1463 is outside the Manston hangars, about to depart.

This Bristol Scout served for six months with the War Flight in 1917 and is a typical example of the fighter aeroplane employed in the mid-war years for Home Defence operations against German bombers and Zeppelins. As the picture shows it was armed with one Lewis machine-gun, and in this case carried extra ammunition magazines in streamlined containers on the fuselage side.

Yet another requisitioned property at Manston. This pre-First World War residence was located approximately where the present-day squash court stands but has long since been demolished. At the time of our photograph it was used by officers of the camp who clearly had no trouble in finding parking spaces for their cars.

Refuelling a Handley Page at Manston, 1917. This particular machine was being prepared for its flight to France where it was destined to join No. 7 Squadron, RNAS. The supply of these aeroplanes and their crews was an important function of Manston and was in full operation by the time this photograph was taken in July. Note the chain-driven, solid-tyred lorry in use – a contrast to the massive petrol-bowsers of the Second World War.

Sopwith Triplane, N.5382, *The Ooslumbird,* was one of the better performance fighters received by the War Flight, Manston, where it served in the latter half of 1917. Records show that it flew many Home Defence sorties in the hands of various pilots of the unit and on 7 July 1917 its pilot, Flt. Sub-Lt. R.H. Daly, destroyed an enemy machine off the Belgian coast.

Early in 1917 another unit, the War School, began to operate at Manston. Its purpose, broadly, was to give RNAS pilots the final stage of training in the fighter role. The instructors and more advanced pupils were sometimes called on to fly on Home Defence patrols. Sopwith Camels of this unit are seen ready for take-off.

Part of the wreckage of the Gotha bomber shot down on 22 August 1917. Considered to be the victim of anti-aircraft batteries, this machine broke up in the air, with pieces falling at Hengrove and, as the picture shows, Vincent's Farm. The crew, Unteroffizier Schildt, Oberleutnant Fulda and Vizefeldwebel Eichelkamp were all killed.

A more detailed view of that section of the Gotha which fell at Vincent's Farm – a wheel, an engine, cowling and part of the wing structure. At the back on the left and standing upright appears to be the framework of the rudder. Eye-witnesses reported that as the machine broke up it also burst into flames.

The scene shortly after dawn on 27 August 1917 in Margate cemetery. The occasion was the burial service with military honours of the German airmen killed at Vincent's Farm five days earlier. The time was chosen in order to avoid possible demonstrations by the citizens. Wg. Cdr. Ross (as he had now become) attended the ceremony with officers and men from Manston and Westgate.

War Flight pilots were heavily involved in the air flights against the fifteen raiders on 22 August. One of the successful combatants was Flt. Lt. A.F. Brandon from the Orange Free State, posing here with a Sopwith Camel he flew that day. With pilots from Dover and Walmer he shared in the destruction of Gotha 663/16 which crashed in the sea three-quarters of a mile off Margate, with only its gunner, Unteroffizier Schneider, surviving.

When the remains of the Vincent's Farm Gotha and those of 663/16 were released by the authorities, a considerable amount of wreckage was turned over to civilian organizations for sale to the public as souvenirs, the money being given to local charities. RNAS personnel at Manston are seen loading lorries with material for the scheme.

It was the practice in the British air services to demonstrate examples of enemy aeroplanes captured in flying condition by visits to some UK aerodromes. This Albatros D.III visited Manston during such a tour. In German service it had been flown by Leutnant Simon of Jasta 11, until his capture on 4 June 1917.

A group of the more prominent pilots at Manston, late 1917/early 1918. Third from left is Sqn. Cdr. C.H. Butler of the War Flight. Fourth from left is Sqn. Cdr. L.S. Breadner and to his left is D.M.B. Galbraith. All three had distinguished flying careers in the First World War and Breadner became Chief of the Air Staff of the Royal Canadian Air Force in the Second World War. The Sopwith Camel belonged to the War School, then commanded by Breadner.

The night of 22/23 December 1917 saw the arrival of another Gotha in Thanet, though not as a result of any warlike action by British air or ground defences. Returning from an attempted raid, the bomber suffered engine trouble, which eventually caused it to land behind what is now Hartsdown County Secondary School.

As this and the preceding photograph show, the crew of the Hartsdown Gotha very effectively destroyed their machine by firing signal flares into it. They were Unteroffizier Hoffman (pilot), Leutnant Dobrick (observer) and Vizefeldwebel Klaus (gunner) of Bogohl 3, based near Ghent, Belgium. For them, as prisoners-of-war, the First World War was over.

The expansion of Manston is well illustrated in this view of the buildings under construction in the Main Camp. Taken in early 1918 from 1,500 ft it shows, from south to north (top of the picture), the major part of the office and domestic site that developed so rapidly about this time, the result of decisions to make Manston a large-scale training base.

In January 1918 work on the Officers' Mess and quarters was reaching its final stage, as our photograph confirms. The building was, in fact, already occupied by permanent staff and some pupils, five of whom are pictured. From the left: Flight Sub-Lieutenants Sutherland, Sprowle, Bradley, Dawson and Cowan – who were attending a War School course en route to active service.

The veranda of the Officers' Mess, Manston, June 1918. An interesting feature to note is the modest attempt to camouflage the higher part of the building. Although considerable changes have been made to the original block over the years much of it remains and is in use to this day, albeit for other purposes.

The Main Camp and cross-roads area of Manston taken in early 1918. In contrast with the previous photograph the construction work appears largely to have been completed. The canvas hangars at centre right house the DH.4 School, a sub-unit of the training establishment, for pilots destined to fly that type on operations.

A line-up of Sopwith Camels of the landplane element of No. 219 Squadron. On the formation of the RAF on 1 April 1918, the seaplane unit at Westgate and its landplanes at Manston became No. 219 Squadron, RAF. These Camel fighters provided the necessary escorts for the seaplanes and anti-submarine DH.9 and 9A types operating from Manston, which were targets of German naval air service fighters from Zeebrugge.

Capt. G. Preen, one of the instructors of No. 203 Training Depot Station, Manston, June 1918. No. 203 TDS was a sizeable unit whose function was to give the later stages of training to pilots who would eventually fly day-bomber machines. Typical of the type is this DH.9, complete with pupil, all set for a practice sortie after a briefing by Preen.

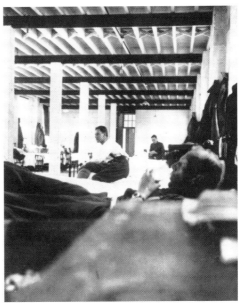

The sleeping quarters of pupils of No. 203 TDS at Manston, June 1918. The scene differs in no way from the trainees' accommodation provided for the same purpose at flying schools of the RAF during the Second World War. Before this building's completion only a short time before, huts or tents had served to house pupils. The original print has the note: 'Wickham (foreground) has a wee drappie!'

The DH.9A, developed from the 9, was the last and most up-to-date type to equip No. 219 Squadron in the last days of the First World War. Engaged on the same duties as its predecessor, it had a much enhanced performance because of the far more powerful engine fitted – either the 375 hp Rolls Royce or the American 'Liberty' of 400 hp. The DH.9A shown outside the Manston hangars was built under sub-contract by Westland Aircraft Works, Yeovil.

Pilots and observers of landplane flights of No. 219 Squadron, late 1918. Behind the group is a Sopwith Camel of the escort flight. The Sidcot flying suit is prominent among those in the front row and, indeed, this overall with its fur collar was widely used up to the Second World War. Lifejackets, forerunners of the famous 'Mae West' of a later war, indicate the over-sea nature of the flights.

This closer view of a DH.9 of No. 219 Squadron shows it to be fully prepared for its next patrol, bombed-up and the gunner's Lewis machine-gun already surmounted. A large and extended exhaust pipe has been fitted to carry the fumes below and clear of the crew who required clear visibility conditions while submarine-hunting.

A selection of the heavy vehicles used by the Aerodrome Construction Corps in building the 'sunken' hangars at Alland Grange, Manston. Leyland and Foden (steam) lorries are prominent in the line-up. The ACC of the Royal Navy specialized in the preparation of aerodromes. Three more of these hangars, constructed by the Royal Engineers, were commenced but cancelled at the Armistice.

The close proximity of the German bomber bases, only 90 miles distant, and the presence of very active and aggressive naval flying units of the German navy encouraged the authorities here to explore safer methods of hangaring Manston's aeroplanes. This aimed at removing them from the risk of surface bomb-blast by using sunken hangars, as illustrated.

Although five such hangars were scheduled only the two near Alland Grange approached completion, so none could be used before the war ended in November 1918. This photograph, taken in August 1918, shows the appearance of such a hangar when almost finished. The preceding print reveals the block walls, steel frame and roof construction, and also the corrugated iron sheet cladding.

From War to Peace – to Crisis: 1919–1938

An aerial view of Manston looking north-west towards Westgate, 1930s.

Bristol Fighter F.4717, another reconditioned machine of First World War vintage, which eventually went to No. 2 Squadron at Manston in April 1926 and served with them until September 1928. It was one of a contract for 700 of the type, known as Bristols, ordered in February 1918 from the British & Colonial Aeroplane Co.

An ex-South Eastern & Chatham Railway 'O' Class locomotive No. 422, which worked the 3¼ mile line between Birchington and Manston Camp. The line was laid in July 1919 and finally closed in 1926.

RAF Manston terminus of the Birchington–Manston spur line, early 1920s. The photograph shows the water tank and buffer stops, and is looking west.

Power station and platform of the spur line, Manston. This recent photograph shows the buildings still in situ, now being used by the RAF Manston Car Club.

Inspection by Air Marshal Sir Hugh Trenchard, February 1921. The march-past at the Station Headquarters Buildings (now demolished) approximately opposite where the Spitfire Museum now stands. The building with the veranda was the first of the camp's permanent buildings to be completed (in 1917).

Air Marshal Sir Hugh Trenchard inspecting members of staff from the School of Technical Training, 22 February 1921.

Inspection by Air Marshal Sir Hugh Trenchard on the Camp parade ground, 22 February 1921. Trenchard was then Chief of the Air Staff and popularly known as the 'Father of the Royal Air Force'.

Avro 504K of the Cornwall Aviation Company (run by Capt. Percival Phillips DFC), see here giving pleasure flights at Chapel Hill, Margate, 1928. The aircraft was finished in pillar box red. The company operated from 1924 to 1933. By the time he died in 1939 it is thought Phillips had carried over 91,000 passengers, most of them in this machine, G–EBIZ, which continued flying until August 1935.

Margate clock tower and seafront taken from the four-engined V/1500 'Super' Handley Page F7139 en route from London to Madrid (via Manston) on 6 May 1919. It was captained by Maj. C. Darley and wrecked in the sea at Biarritz on 29 May on its return flight from Spain.

An aerial view of the Margate Winter Gardens and seafront taken from a Short 184 seaplane operating from Westgate, *c.* 1919.

Aerial view of Manston village, *c.* 1920.

A formation of Bristol Fighters of No. 2 Squadron over RAF Manston. The photograph dates from the late 1920s. No. 2 Squadron served at Manston on and off for eleven years.

A solemn occasion: the unveiling of the Manston war memorial by Officer Commanding Wg. Cdr. Primrose in Manston village, *c.* 1921.

An aerial view of the harbour and old town area of Margate, taken from a Short 184 seaplane operating from Westgate, *c.* 1919.

53

The three crew members of Vickers Vimy F9157 are laid to rest, 3 October 1921. The aircraft (a twin-engined bomber) crashed due to engine failure following take-off. Vimy F9157 served with No. 6 FTS at the time of the accident.

Manston MT corner. These buildings, long since removed, were part of the School of Technical Training complex and stood in the area now occupied by the new officers' married quarters. The road to the right leads to Birchington and that to the left to Minster. The photographer was positioned on the road that crosses the aerodrome.

The Volunteer Pipe Band, which was formed at RAF Manston in 1923. Perhaps there was a sizeable contingent of Scots among the Manston personnel in 1923. The band are standing on what is now the Sergeants' Mess car-park.

Bristol Fighters of No. 2 Squadron. The squadron was based at Manston from March 1924 to April 1927, moving to China (Shanghai) in that year. The squadron later returned to Manston. One can just make out the squadron marking on the fuselage, comprising two red rings enclosing another colour to indicate individual flights. No. 2 Squadron re-equipped with Atlas aircraft in December 1929.

A Bristol Fighter of No. 2 Squadron and squadron personnel at Okehampton, Devon, during the annual summer exercise camp in which squadrons were deployed away from their base. The photograph was taken in 1925.

F.4717 – one of a batch of 700 machines. Built by the Bristol & Colonial Aeroplane Co., F.4717 served with No. 2 Squadron from April 1926 to September 1928. The Bristol Fighter was one of the First World War designs that gave long first-line service to the RAF from 1917 to 1932, and to training units for even longer. It had been designed in 1916.

Yet another Bristol Fighter comes to grief, a No. 2 Squadron machine. Interested ground crew survey the wreckage. A great many of the RAF's machines in the 1920s–30s were reconditioned First World War products. This was the direct result of the severe financial constraints imposed on the Service in those years.

A No. 9 Squadron Vickers Virginia clears the hangar on its approach, 1929.

Avro 504K, G–EBIZ of the Cornwall Aviation Company about to take off from Chapel Hill, Margate, 1928. There were many small operators in this business and in the early 1920s some used Manston as their base of operations.

No. 500 Squadron (County of Kent) was based at Manston from March 1931 to January 1936. Flying and ground crews or (trainee) officers of the Squadron in front of one of their Vickers Virginia machines.

'B' Flight, No. 9 Squadron, 8 March 1926. The squadron was equipped with Mk. VI Virginias from September 1924 to November 1930 – one of the earlier marks of Virginia flown by this unit.

Ground crew and Bristol Fighter of No. 2 Squadron, 1925. This aircraft was one of a batch (215 in number) built in 1920–1. Note the squadron marking, round the rear fuselage, of two red bands with a central band in the individual colour of the flight. The photograph is of a machine of 'C' Flight, which had a blue central band.

RCM Pink. As Wing Commander of No. 2 (India) Wing he conducted what became known as 'Pink's War' against rebel tribes in Waziristan from March to May 1925. The photograph shows him at that time after a flight in the region. Pink was CO at RAF Manston from May 1929 to October 1931. He died in the RAF hospital, Halton on 7 March 1932. Known as a very popular and extremely capable officer, he was destined for the highest ranks in a brilliant career. His ashes were scattered at RAF Manston.

Ground crew and DH.9A of No. 605 (County of Warwick) Squadron, Royal Auxiliary Air Force on annual summer camp from Castle Bromwich, at Manston during the late 1920s. The squadron operated DH.9As from October 1926 to April 1930.

Vickers Virginias of No. 9 Squadron join in the tea-party and startle the guests at a Manston local Air Day during the late 1920s.

Aerial view of the admin and workshop area in the 1920s.

A pilot and ground staff of 'A' Flight, No. 500 Squadron (County of Kent) and a Vickers Virginia. Virginias served with No. 9 Squadron, No. 7 Squadron and No. 58 as well as No. 500 Squadron.

All hands to the prop. Members of the Oxford University Air Squadron strain to start up a squadron Avro 504N, 1933.

A No. 500 Squadron (County of Kent) Vickers Virginia (*Deal Castle*) being 'bombed-up' during a night exercise. No. 500 Squadron moved to Detling in September 1938. The 500 series were called Special Reserve Squadrons and were not officially part of the Royal Auxiliary Air Force until July 1937.

Naming ceremony of Vickers Virginia *Isle of Thanet* by the then Mayor of Ramsgate, Alderman E.E. Dye, on 4 June 1931. This aircraft served with No. 500 Squadron (County of Kent).

Manston sports team, 1932–3. Sports, especially team games, have always been a significant part of life in the RAF. Manston has been a good example of this, and over the years has produced many prize-winning teams in various sports both within the Service and against civilian opponents. In the centre is a group of officers, complete with CO, with either the Adjutant or Sports Officer on his left.

Manston sports day, early 1930s. This sports ground was laid out on the northern section of the aerodrome and adjacent to the Margate road. Most of the main camp is seen in the background.

King's Birthday Parade, 1930s. The parade with the troops drawn up in ranks was held on the sports ground depicted on the previous page.

Hawker Audax Mk 1, No. 2 Squadron, *c*. 1934. Following a long spell of service flying Bristol Fighters, the squadron re-equipped with Atlas aeroplanes from December 1929 to May 1933 before acquiring the Hawker Audax, which remained in use until November 1937. Note that the squadron marking had become a triangle.

No. 2 Squadron, *c*. 1933. Officers and NCOs of the squadron can be seen, of whom five are wearing decorations and/or campaign medals. The squadron leader (front right) is thought to be P.F. Fullard DSO, MC, AFC, a very distinguished fighter pilot during the First World War.

Armstrong Whitworth Atlas aircraft of No. 2 Squadron in flight, 1930.

A common sight during the late 1920s: Vickers Virginias from No. 9 Squadron fly over the Isle of Thanet.

Vickers Virginias of No. 9 Squadron, *c.* 1929.

A No. 2 Squadron Armstrong Whitworth Atlas, June 1930. The Atlas first entered service with the RAF in October 1927. No. 2 Squadron was re-equipped with the Atlas in December 1929.

Accidents will happen: a Vickers Virginia after a forced landing, Manston, *c.* 1931.

No. 2 Squadron over Thanet. This is a composite photograph that was probably created by the photographic section to be used on Christmas cards and the like.

An informal snap of one of the pilots and some of the ground crew of No. 2 Squadron, Manston. The aircraft in the background is a Hawker Audax.

An interior shot of the airmen's billets, all ready for inspection with stacked beds, biscuits, wall lockers, bedside lockers and Macdonald folding beds, 1932.

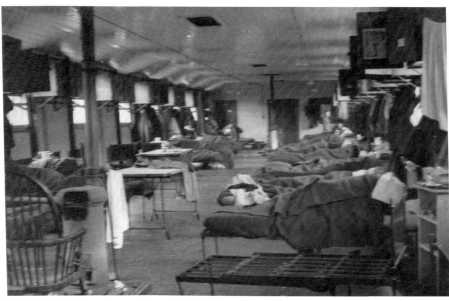

The interior of an airmen's hut, *c.* 1939. In the foreground is a Macdonald folding bed. The hut's main source of heat was of course the ubiquitous coke stove.

Alan Cobham (third from right) learned to fly in the RAF at Manston in 1918. Post-war he engaged in 'barnstorming' round the UK. In 1932 he formed the National Aviation Day Display which toured the British Isles and greatly popularized aviation. He is seen here with other pilots of his 'Circus' in 1932. He was to become Sir Alan Cobham in later years and was mainly responsible for the development of mid-air refuelling.

An aerial view of RAF Manston, 1932. Many of the buildings seen in this photograph were to succumb to the Luftwaffe attacks of 1940.

Edward Hillman of Hillman Airways being congratulated by the Mayor of Ramsgate after the first flight into RAF Manston by Hillman Airways, 1932. The aircraft is a Fox Moth. The journey time from Romford to Manston was twenty-three minutes.

Stand by your vehicles: members of the Motor Transport Section, 1932.

A visiting Westland Wapiti of No. 603 Squadron (City of Edinburgh), *c.* 1933.
Although never based at or detached to Manston it is entirely possible that one of 603's
aircraft paid a visit for a 'one-off' reason. No. 603 Squadron was based at Turnhouse,
Scotland and flew Wapitis from March 1930 to March 1934.

Manston, c. 1933. These are probably trainees of the Oxford University Air Squadron with an Avro 504N. They were regular visitors to Manston for their summer camp and annual training in the 1930s.

The last open cockpit fighter to see service with the RAF was the Gloster Gauntlet, seen here at a pre-war Open Day.

Wings of the weird and wonderful: a Westland Pterodactyl Mk. V, K.2770, visiting Manston on an Open or Air Day along with a number of other 'strangers', c. 1934.

A flight of Fairey Gordons drop into Manston during the mid-1930s. The Gordon remained in RAF service throughout the 1930s until the outbreak of the Second World War in 1939.

A visiting Westland Wallace samples the delights of RAF Manston, *c.* 1935. The Wallace was to remain in RAF service until it was retired in 1943.

Ground crew working on a Hawker Hind of No. 500 Squadron (County of Kent). The Hind was a development of the earlier Hawker Hart. It was powered by a Rolls Royce Kestrel engine that gave the aircraft a maximum speed of 192 mph.

Manston East Camp, looking to the north-west towards Westgate, 1930s. The huts behind the hangars, originally built in 1916, have now become airmen's married quarters (note washing lines). At the top of the picture can be seen the sports pavilion. One can also see the new concrete apron freshly laid in front of the hangars.

Saro Cloud of No. 48 Squadron. These aircraft formed part of 'B' Flight of the Seaplane Training Squadron based at Calshot and were attached to Manston for six months. The type's primary function was the training of pilots in handling flying boats.

No. 48 Squadron Avro Anson Mk. 1, *c.* 1937. The squadron was based at Manston from March 1936, moving to Eastchurch in September 1938. Manston received Ansons from the first production batch when they were issued to No. 48 Squadron in March 1936.

Aerial view of RAF Manston, giving an excellent view of Ponce's Farm, School of Technical Training, hangars and the adjacent railway terminal, mid-1930s.

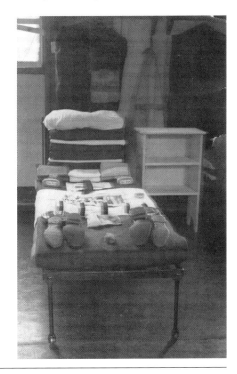

Kit inspection, 1939. Boxed blankets, folded towels and shining boots are the order of the day, all mounted on a Macdonald bed. Woe betide the airman if the inspecting officer found just a speck of dust.

Safely tucked in – No. 48 Squadron Ansons. This method of hangaring aeroplanes was abandoned soon after the outbreak of the Second World War when dispersal became the order of the day. Note the heating duct along the centre sections of the roof. The hangar was sited within the East Camp area.

A line up of No. 48 Squadron Avro Ansons, c. 1937. The CO of No. 48 Squadron at this time was Sqn. Ldr. T.A. Langford-Sainsbury. This line-up stretches across the aerodrome from East Camp in a south-westerly direction. In the background you can just make out the MT building and HQ complex.

SECTION THREE

The Second Conflict:
1939–1945

A makeshift armoured car mounting a First World War vintage Lewis gun, for basic airfield defence. It was part of Manston's mobile defence force in 1940.

A Vickers Wellington of No. 3 GRU fitted with a degaussing ring used to detonate magnetic mines. The photograph dates from late 1939 when this unit was based at Manston.

A grand bunch of lads known as the 'Four Marx Brothers': Reg, Shorty, Stan and Bill, who were all serving at Manston in 1940. Perhaps someone can supply details about these lads in blue.

The late Sqn. Ldr. Tollemache, whose brave action on the night of 11 March 1940 led to the award of the Empire Gallantry Medal (later known as the George Cross). The Blenheim (L6682) he was piloting crashed on the approach to RAF Manston, and Tollemache returned to his burning aircraft in a vain attempt to rescue Lt. Sperling of the Welsh Guards, a passenger in the Blenheim.

Bristol Blenheim Z5722, late of No. 600 Squadron. This aeroplane became the personal mount of the OC No. 68 Squadron, Wg. Cdr. the Hon Max Aitken DFC. Z5722 served with No. 600 Squadron when at Manston in 1940.

A Heinkel HE111 of 6/KG4 spread across the beach at Sacketts Gap, Margate, Wednesday 19 June 1940. Damaged by fire from FO Ball of No. 19 Squadron over Colchester the German bomber only just made it across the Estuary. Fw. Reitzig died while trying to bale out. The rest of the crew ended up as POWs.

RAF personnel inspecting a bomb crater, perhaps after one of the severe August 1940 raids. This is a very rare photograph indeed, as very few images survive of Manston during the Battle of Britain period.

Defiants of No. 264 Squadron in formation over Thanet. Powered by a Rolls Royce Merlin and armed with a powered turret mounting four .303 machine-guns, which seemed all conquering during early combat sorties, the Defiant soon fell prey to German fighters armed with a forward firing armament and was withdrawn from daylight operations in August 1940.

Members of No. 264 Squadron. The squadron was decimated while operating from Manston. Sqn. Ldr. P.A. Hunter can be seen standing third from the left. Philip Hunter and his gunner Fred King were killed during combat operations over the Channel on 24 August 1940. The last daytime sortie carried out by No. 264 Squadron was on Wednesday 28 August 1940.

Soldiers proudly show off the remains of a Luftwaffe bomb. The original caption states that the photograph was taken at the Spurgeons Home, Birchington, 1940. It also claims that this was the first 'whistling bomb' dropped on Kent.

Opposite: Resplendent in flying clothing, Tim Smith of No. 600 Squadron takes a well-earned respite after a sortie. Squadron Blenheims can be seen in the background.

Manston's 130-stone tug-of-war team, 1939. From left to right: J. McLean, J. Wilkinson, J. Kinlock, F. Ford, I. Reid, T. Burgess, G. Ellis, K. Hope, Sgt. Bunyan, F. Palmer, Flt. Lt. Walker, Grp. Capt. Strugnel, Sgt. Robinson, Sgt. Northwood and G.F. Imrie.

An important visitor chats with members of No. 615 Squadron, 28 August 1940. Winston Churchill inspects the station and 615, who at that time had a detachment operating from Manston flying Gloster Gladiators (the squadron was later re-equipped with Hurricanes).

Unteroffizier Schulte's war ended when his Bf109E–4 force-landed at Vincents Farm, Manston on 6 September 1940. The aircraft was later used to raise money for various war charities.

Heinkel HE111 Werk Nummer 2782 of 6/KG53 ended up in a field of ripe cabbages on 30 August 1940, after being damaged by pilots of No. 242 Squadron.

Wounded in the head, Oberlt. Bartels managed to force-land his aircraft at Northdown, Margate on Wednesday 24 July 1940. The Bf109E–1 (Werk Nummer 6296) was later used to raise money for the 'County' Spitfire Fund. Oberlt. Bartels was later repatriated in 1943.

Yet another Luftwaffe aircraft falls to the guns of the RAF, Monday 12 August 1940. At 6 p.m. Oberlt. Drehs of III/JG54 crash landed his Bf109E–4 on farmland at Hengrove midway between Margate and Manston.

Drehs' aircraft is taken away for further examination.

A No. 74 Squadron Mk. IIA Spitfire awaits the order to scramble, Manston, February 1941. In the background is the burnt-out hangar, which was destroyed during the August 1940 raids on the station.

Pilots of No. 92 East India Squadron with their scoreboard, February 1941. Seated in the cockpit of one of the squadron's Spitfires is Brian Kingcombe, a leading figure within the squadron. On Wednesday 5 February 1941 PO Fokes of No. 92 Squadron shot down one of the last Ju87s (Stuka) to fall on British soil as it approached Manston.

A Bell Aircobra Mk. 1 in flight. This aircraft (AH573) later served with No. 601 Squadron at Manston in 1941.

Members of No. 92 Squadron, Manston, January 1941. Highly successful during the Battle of Britain under the command of Johnny Kent, No. 92 Squadron spent only a short time operating from Manston (January to February 1941).

A 3-in gun of First World War vintage forms part of RAF Manston's anti-aircraft defences during the early days of the Second World War. The gun in the photograph was located at Telegraph Hill, Minster, adjacent to 'Smuggler's Leap'.

Standing before the entrance of the Officers' Mess at Doone House, Westgate, are General de Gaulle and Air Vice Marshal Leigh-Mallory.

The General takes the salute from members of No. 615 Squadron. Founder of the Free French movement in Britain during the war, de Gaulle was French President from 1959 to 1969.

The General chats with Free French pilots of No. 615 Squadron. Standing on the left and just behind de Gaulle is Phillipe de Scitivaux, a French pilot.

General de Gaulle being welcomed to RAF Manston, 29 October 1941. The building in the background is now used by the ATC as an accommodation block.

General de Gaulle stops to chat to Phillipe de Scitivaux during his visit to No. 615 Squadron.

General de Gaulle lunching with Free French pilots at the Officers' Mess, Doone House, Westgate.

The remains of PO Chester's Spitfire Mk. II, P7854 of No. 74 Squadron, which crashed on the parade ground at Manston after attempting a 'victory roll', 10 April 1941. Chester had just shot down a Bf109E of 11/JG51 over Canterbury. The German crashed on Frost Farm, St Nicholas-at-Wade.

Major Helge Mehre DFC, Commanding Officer of No. 331 Norwegian Squadron. Mehre flew four missions from Manston during Operation Jubilee (the Dieppe operation, 19 August 1942) accounting for two Fw190s. Five squadrons flew from Manston during the Dieppe operation, including 174, North Weald Fighter Wing comprising Nos 242 (British), 331 (Norwegian) and 403 (Canadian).

Lt. Cdr. Eugene Esmonde VC, DSO led six Swordfish torpedo bombers of No. 825 Squadron, Fleet Air Arm, from Manston on 12 February 1942 against the German battleships *Scharnhorst*, *Gneisenau* and *Prinz Eugen*. They were to suffer terrible losses, including the death of the gallant Esmonde, who was later awarded a posthumous Victoria Cross for his actions on that fateful day.

On 12 February 1987 RAF Manston welcomed four survivors of the Swordfish attack on the German battleships, forty-five years later to the day. Left to right: Cdr. E. Lee DSO, RN (rtd), Lt. Cdr. C.M. Kingsmill DSO, VRD, RNR (rtd), the late Grp. Capt. Tom Gleave CBE, RAF (rtd), Station Commander, RAF Manston, 1942, Leading Airman D.A. Bunce RN (rtd), Lt. Cdr. R. McC. Samples CMG, DSO, RN (rtd).

A Fairey Swordfish biplane torpedo bomber of the type used during the attack on the German battleships during the 'Channel Dash'. With a top speed in the region of 138 mph, and armed with one forward firing .303 machine-gun and a .303 Lewis gun in the aft cockpit, the Swordfish was no match for the battleships' defences and Luftwaffe fighters.

'The Sea Shall Not Have Them': the moment when a young airman finds rescue at hand after ditching in the cold waters of the English Channel. In this case HSL 149 is picking up Flt. Sgt. Randle of No. 111 Squadron off North Foreland, 21 July 1942.

Launch No. 149 makes a run for its home port after plucking yet another Allied airman from a watery grave. This particular vessel was based at Ramsgate and was struck off charge in May 1957.

No. 137 Squadron Westland Whirlwinds lined up at Manston, *c.* 1942.

Whirlwind Mk. 1, serial number P7055, 1943. This particular aircraft was scrapped on 30 September 1944.

A Whirlwind of No. 137 Squadron, 1943. Powered by Rolls Royce Peregrine engines, and with a strong cannon armament, the Whirlwind proved itself in the ground attack role while operating from Manston.

A Westland Whirlwind of No. 137 Squadron awaiting the next sortie, 1943. The squadron carried out operations from Manston from September 1942 to June 1943.

Flt. Lt. the Baron Jean De Selys Longchamps DFC. A Belgian baron and second cousin to the King of Belgium, Longchamps was killed while serving with No. 3 Squadron, flying Typhoon EJ950. His aircraft crashed on its approach before landing.

The concentrated roar of Sabre engines echoes across the airfield as No. 609 Squadron prepares for yet another tactical operation over occupied Europe in mid-1943.

No. 609 Squadron form up for take-off. The Hawker Typhoon, powered by a twenty-four cylinder Napier Sabre engine, proved itself in a low-level strike role both before and after D-Day. Armed with four 20-mm cannon the Typhoon became an awesome adversary in the close quarter air combat over occupied Europe.

Sqn. Ldr. Roland (Bee) Beamont (left) and Sqn. Ldr. Alec Ingle handing over No. 609 Squadron, May 1943.

Sir Archibald Sinclair, Secretary for Air, chatting with members of No. 609 Squadron. On the left of Sir Archibald (in trench coat), with his hands on hips, is Sqn. Ldr. R.P. Beamont DFC, the 22-year-old Commanding Officer of No. 609 Squadron. He was awarded a well-deserved DSO in May 1943.

The side panel from Wg. Cdr. Beamont's Typhoon with the motto of No. 609 Squadron (West Riding). This is now on display in the Air Historical Branch, London.

Pilots of No. 609 Squadron, with the squadron mascot 'Wing Commander de Goat'. From left to right: Zeigler, Comson, CO Beamont, Lallemond, Raw (holding up de Goat), Haabjoern, Stark, Rolek, Jackson and Geerts.

A No. 609 Squadron Typhoon about to set out on a tactical mission, 1943. The aircraft is being seen off by the ground crew plus one or two WAAFs, who have taken the trouble to stick saving stamps all over the 500 lb bomb slung beneath the aircraft.

Boston Mk. IIIs of No. 107 Squadron, based at Hartfordbridge, on a flying visit to Manston, 1943.

The Boeing B-17 Flying Fortress, a durable and well-armed aircraft. Between 1942 and 1945, during the daylight bombing offensive against Hitler's Reich, many damaged B-17s landed at Manston.

A North American Mitchell Mk. II, serial FL167, of No. 98 Squadron suffered a forced landing at Manston on 10 June 1943, after being hit by flak over the target. No. 98 Squadron was operating from Foulsham against communications centres and airfields.

Believed by some to be the most elegant bomber of the Second World War, the Martin B.26 Marauder served with distinction. Powered by two Double Wasp radial engines, the Marauder was a frequent visitor to Manston during the American daylight bombing offensive.

North American P.51D Mustang. Together with the P.38 Lightning and the P.47 Thunderbolt, these provided the backbone of the 8th Army Air Force fighter strength during the Second World War. Quite a few P.51s force-landed at Manston after providing cover to American bombers during daylight operations.

1944 proved to be a busy year for American aircraft force-landing at Manston. This P.47D, serial number 225690, serving with No. 84 Fighter Squadron, 78 Fighter Group based at Duxford, has found a safe haven on the airfield.

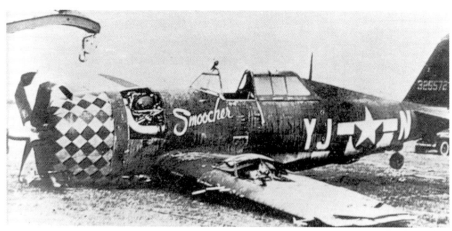

P.47D, 325572, sustained major damage after a forced landing at Manston, 1944. The aircraft carries the markings of the 353rd Fighter Group, based at Raydon. The yellow and black checker-board pattern extended back to the cowling shutters.

Yet another P.47D Thunderbolt or 'Jug' meets its demise after ploughing into a building at Manston, 1944. This aircraft served with No. 487 Fighter Squadron, 352 Fighter Group based at Bodney.

A B.24 Liberator of the 448th Bomb Group operating out of Seething. On 24 March 1945 a B.24 from this unit was abandoned over Manston. All the crew members baled out as the aircraft crashed in fields adjacent to the airfield.

Ground crew and Spitfire Mk. IX of No. 504 Squadron, 1944.

Manston's Intelligence Hut sited on the Main Camp side of the airfield. It was the home of the Station Intelligence Officer, H.J. Smith ('Smithy') from August 1940 to March 1943. Many famous pilots such as 'Sailor' Malan, Al Deere, Max Aitken, Stanford-Tuck, Whitney Straight and Johnny Kent visited 'Smithy' in his den. Other famous visitors included Winston Churchill and 'Clemmie', General Montgomery and Lord Trenchard.

Two members of No. 504 Squadron – on the left Flt. Lt. Steele and on the right Flt. Lt. Kenneth William Bishop. Ken Bishop was killed on 31 August 1944 while air-testing Spitfire PL222. The aircraft crashed close to the beach at Sandwich.

Members of No. 504 Squadron taking in the August sunshine, Manston 1944. Flt. Lt. Bishop is seated and wearing his 'Mae West'. An experienced pilot, Ken was on his second tour when killed flying Spitfire PL222.

A happy snap taken at 'Rusty' Steele's wedding, July 1944. Flt. Lt. 'Bish' Bishop, acting as best man, is about to put money into the gentleman's cap after leaving the church. A few weeks later 'Bish' Bishop was to make his last flight.

Members of No. 504 Squadron, Manston, August 1944. The squadron later moved to Hawkinge, remaining there until February 1945.

Armstrong Whitworth AW 41 Albemarle taking off with a Horsa glider in tow and heading for the drop zone at Arnhem, 17 September 1944. A four-seat transport and glider tug, the Albemarle came into its own during operation Market Garden, the assault on the Rhine bridges at Arnhem on 17 and 18 September 1944.

The Albemarle clears the runway, passing over the mass of aircraft awaiting their turn to take off.

Meteor Mk. I standing on the PSP hardstanding located on the south side of the airfield. No. 616 Squadron received its first Meteors in July 1944. Armed with four 20-mm cannon the Meteor packed quite a punch. Coupled with a top speed of 415 mph and a service ceiling of 40,000 ft, the Meteor was the forerunner of today's modern jet fighters.

Avro Lancasters being dismantled by 54 Maintenance Unit on the 'Loop', 1945.

An Albemarle of No. 297 Squadron, *c.* 1944.

Another view of Avro Lancasters being dismantled by 54 Maintenance Unit on the 'Loop', 1945.

No. 616 Squadron Meteor Mk. Is lined up at Manston. The photograph was taken on 4 January 1945. The Meteor proved itself during the V1 (Doodlebug) offensive in mid-1944.

A Lancaster makes a safe landing, using FIDO. FIDO (Fog Intensive Dispersal Operation) equipment had been installed on fifteen airfields within the UK, at Manston during the later stages of the Second World War. The photograph was taken at RAF Graveley, but it does show the effect of the system at 'full burn'.

Personnel prepare to activate the system perparatory to a 'burn'.

The original fuel tanks for the FIDO system. They are still in situ and now form part of the Jentex oil company complex.

Two legendary fighter pilots, Grp. Capt. Sir Douglas Bader and Wg. Cdr. Robert Stanford-Tuck, standing next to TB 752, the 'Manston Spitfire'. The Spitfire is still with us in the Spitfire and Hurricane Museum, Manston, but both pilots have now sadly passed away.

Two wartime views of the Manston bomb dump, 1945.

A present-day view of the old Sergeants' Mess in Westgate. The Mess moved from Manston for the duration of the Second World War.

Doone House, used by the RAF as an Officers' Mess during the Second World War. The building can still be seen today, in Canterbury Road, Westgate.

Remains of the Foreness CHL Radar Station. The photograph was taken in 1968 after the bulk of the equipment and buildings had been removed.

The Old Charles pub, Cliftonville, Margate, a favourite haunt for pilots and ground crews from RAF Manston during the war years. It was renowned for its extended drinking hours and down to earth hospitality.

A modified Dakota of No. 77 Squadron standing by to take part of No. 26 'stick' Parachute Regiment to their drop zone during Exercise Longstop, 1947. The aircrew standing in the door-hatch are: top right, Flt. Lt. Alfie Burt; bottom left, WO Ron Rand. Longstop was one of the largest post-war exercises involving ground and air forces. The photograph was taken at the Loop, 1947.

Ground crew and Dakota of No. 77 Squadron, 1947.

The final resting place for numerous Luftwaffe aircrew shot down over East Kent and the approaches to RAF Manston was the German war graves section of Margate cemetery.

SECTION FOUR
The American Years: 1950–1958

A line-up of F84E Thunderjets of the 406th Fighter Bomber Wing, *c.* 1954.

Fred Lincoln shooting a line on top of the tower, having just been promoted to temp SATCO (Senior Air Traffic Control Officer), summer 1954.

The Homer radio beacon, an aid to navigation, 1952.

The old wartime control tower 1952, complete with the only remaining bomb crater.

A member of the Air Traffic Control staff performing his duties. Taken from the top of the control tower, this photograph takes in the accommodation and administration buildings that made up the station in the 1950s.

The Prospect Inn, a haven for the hard-pressed airman and only a short walk from the airfield. The venue now has Grade 2 Listed status.

Airfield Control caravan, at the end of Runway 29, June 1954.

The main Guard Room, a place to strike fear into the hearts of airmen on the station, mid-1950s. 'Bulled' boots and white webbing were the hallmark of the RAF policeman.

The control tower, focal point of any airfield and the home of Air Traffic Control, *c*. 1950.

'Where's the NAAFI then?' Fred Lincoln on the prod for morning 'tuck', spring 1954.

Anti polio vaccine being loaded on to an Avro Anson during the Hull polio epidemic, October 1961.

North American F-86 Sabre shows off its clean lines on one of the Manston hardstandings, *c.* 1953.

F-86 Sabres glint in the late afternoon sun, mid-1950s. The nearest aircraft to the camera has extended air brakes.

RAF Manston, looking east-south-east, *c*. 1955.

Ground crew toil on an F-84 Thunderjet, 1953.

Republic F-84 Thunderjets, *c.* 1954.

North American F-86D, *c.* 1956. Note the large radome in the nose above the jet intake.

A brace of SA-16 Albatross amphibians make up part of the 9th Air Sea Rescue Squadron USAF, which operated from Manston in the 1950s.

'Hands Across the Sea.' Sgt. Walt Wilson with an English friend standing in front of the radio shack, 1952.

Ready for anything the Cold War can throw. An American airman in full battle order, complete with M.1 Carbine, 1952.

Sgt. Walt Wilson waiting for the bus at Manston, 1952.

The pall of smoke hanging over the airfield marks the final resting place of a Republic F-84 Thunderjet of the 'Skyblazers' – a team of seven aircraft giving a display on Wednesday 21 May 1952. The pilot, Capt. John Patrick O'Brien, died in the crash. Problems with the American jet engines led to the unprecedented step of calling in Rolls Royce technicians. In time the problems caused by engine failures were solved by the 'boffins' from Rolls.

Workshops used by the USAF, East Camp, *c.* 1952. This is now the site of the Kent International Airport terminal.

A view from the control tower. Note the crash-crew facilities, including fire engines.

A C54 Transport calls in at Manston, mid-1950s.

A KC 97 Tanker of the USAF flies into Manston, *c.* 1955.

An American 'snow drop' (American Air Force policeman) on duty, *c.* 1955.

Ground crew toil on an F-86D Sabre of the 513th Fighter Squadron, 1955.

A TU 104, one of three such aircraft that landed at Manston carrying members of the famous Bolshoi Ballet Company. The aircraft and dancers arrived on 1 October 1956. A fleet of three East Kent coaches took the troupe up to London. These were the very first Russian aircraft to land at Manston.

The Queen Mother flew into Manston in a Viking of the Queen's Flight on Wednesday 23 May 1956. She was en route to Deal where she carried out two engagements. She is seen here chatting to American personnel, who seem to be making the most of this impromptu photo-call.

An F-86 Sabre based at Manston during the mid- to late 1950s.

'There's something about a Nissen Hut.' This view dates from the mid-1950s, the American period.

At 2 a.m. on 27 November 1954 a message was flashed from the Ramsgate coastguard to No. 66 Air Sea Rescue Squadron at Manston. At 9 a.m. a helicopter piloted by Capt. Curtis E. Parkins found the stricken Goodwin lightship wrecked on the deadly sands. On deck there was one survivor, Ronald Murton. The winchman, Airman First Class Elmer Vollman, lifted Murton to safety.

A B17 at rest on the hardstanding at Manston during the mid-1950s.

The stars and stripes lowered for the last time at a simple ceremony, 15 June 1958. This was the end of an era at RAF Manston.

Into the Seventies:
Civil Operations

A Silver City Handley Page Hermes 88-seat airliner and crew. On the right of the photograph is Wg. Cdr. Hugh Kennard, Chairman of Silver City. Four Hermes aircraft together with a number of DC3 Dakotas were transferred to Manston in 1959. From here they continued with passenger inclusive charters and trooping flights worldwide.

A Douglas DC3 Dakota 36-seat airliner of Silver City Airways, 1959.

'Open wide': a Silver City Airways Bristol 170 car carrier. The aircraft could carry three cars and fourteen passengers. Silver City transferred a small part of its expanding car ferry operations to Manston from Lydd (Ferryfield) for service on their Ostend route. Three Bristol 170 Mk. 21 aircraft were utilized for this purpose in 1960. This service did not continue for very long and was re-transferred back to Lydd.

Bristol 170 Mk. 21 operating from Manston, 1960.

Douglas DC4, operated by Air Ferry Ltd, and crew.

Invicta Airways Ltd commenced operations from Manston on 30 March 1962. Before this date considerable work had been carried out in the reconstruction of a passenger terminal building. The result was a very modern terminal and lounge.

Douglas DC4 of Invicta Airways standing in front of what was to be the home of Jet Support, Manston.

Passengers make their way into the original Air Ferry terminal, 1962.

DC4s of Air Ferry Ltd lined up on the tarmac.

A Vickers Viking 36-seat airliner operated by Invicta out of Manston, *c.* 1964.

An evocative air to air photograph of an Invicta Airways Vickers Viscount Type 700 airliner. The first 'revenue' flight by Invicta took place on 20 March 1965. In that year the company took delivery of two Viscounts.

Down and nearly out, 20 April 1967. A Bristol Britannia of British Eagle suffered a complete undercarriage failure and belly-landed on a foam carpet.

A Vickers Vanguard runs up its engines in front of the Invicta Air International hangar. The company changed its name from Invicta Air Cargo Ltd to Invicta International in 1970.

The main operations building, Invicta Airways Ltd, 1970.

Engine overhaul shop, Invicta International, *c.* 1970.

The interior of the Invicta Aircraft Engineering Ltd hangar. Numerous small airlines used this facility for overhauls and other mechanical work. In 1971 Hugh Kennard formed another two companies, Invicta Aircraft Engineering, to service the fleet aircraft and also to carry out technical services for other operators, and Interland Air Services Ltd, a small air taxi company for individual air charter and crew transportation.

A twin-engined Piper Aztec of Interland Air Services Ltd.

Boeing 720B 180-seat passenger airliner, serving with Invicta International. The company purchased two 720Bs from American Airlines in 1973.

A Vickers Vanguard of Invicta Air Cargo being loaded, 1971.

A shot of the interior of the Invicta Air Cargo Freight building and TIR Warehouse, 1977. This section of the building was designated as an Inland Clearance Depot by HM Customs for the handling of TIR (Transport International Routier) vehicles from the Continent, involving 1,000 tons per week.

An aerial view of the civil aviation complex. During the period 1959–80 it was estimated that some two million passengers were carried through Manston together with many thousands of tons of cargo.

Cargo was loaded round the clock. Here a Bristol Britannia is taking on cargo at night.

A Bristol Britannia of Invicta International. This particular aircraft was a cargo variant of the famous airliner.

Two views of the modern Kent International terminal, opened in 1989 by the Duchess of York. The terminal can handle more than 500 passengers an hour.

Acknowledgements

This publication was compiled and written by the following members of RAF Manston History Club, all aviation enthusiasts with a particular interest in Manston's past as an RAF base: Norman Bird, Frank Cheesman, Douglas Cockle, Roy Doherty, Jack Peppiatt and John T. Williams.

The following people and organizations deserve our sincere thanks. If we have missed anyone out we unreservedly apologize.

D.A. Alderton • Miss Bishop • Chaz Bowyer• G.T Bromet
J.M. Bruce/G.S. Leslie Collection • H.A. Buss • H.A. Clayfield
Mrs Clifford • D.G. Collyer • Ken Cox • Alan Day • Roger Freeman
Chris Fright • Leslie Hunt • Members of KAHRS • F.J. Keble
Wg. Cdr. H.C. Kennard DFC (retd) • Joe Kovac • G.E. Livock
Malik Art • Manston Photographic Archive • Margate Museum
Wg. Cdr. Montgomery • Tony Moor • R. Redford • D.B. Robertson
R.P. Ross • M. Twyman • Les Walker • Len Walsham
Geoff Williams Collection • Mrs Joan Wilson • Walt Wilson

RAF
MANSTON
ALBUM

PART TWO

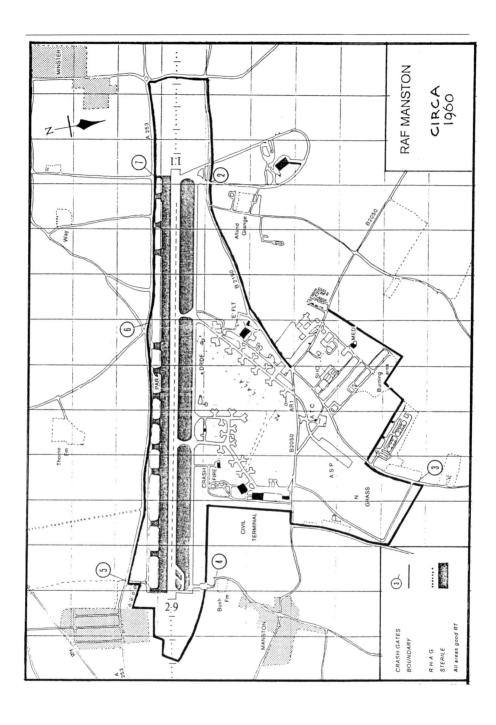

RAF MANSTON

CIRCA 1960

Contents

Foreword

The present infrastructure of RAF Manston is itself a record of its history, with a range of buildings that originate from its very earliest days to some that were constructed during the late eighties. This book portrays a mixture of events at RAF Manston, both significant and routine, which have occurred in and around these buildings. Individually some of the events may appear of little consequence. However, together they help bring to life memories of the station, especially for those who have been associated with it over the years.

Manston is one of the few RAF stations, if not the only one, to have seen continuous service since 1916. Furthermore, its location has been geographically significant, not only during the two world wars but also, because of its proximity to the Continent, during the Cold War when, among other roles, it provided an arrival/departure point for many aircraft in transit between the forces stationed in Germany and the United Kingdom. The station has also hosted a search and rescue helicopter unit, under various guises, since July 1961. After thirty-three years, following a review of the UK search and rescue organization, the most recent unit, 'C' Flight No. 202 Squadron, finally departs to Wattisham in July 1994. It is therefore a particular pleasure for me that some of its activities at Manston are recorded within these pages.

Events at Manston, and specifically during the Battle of Britain, have been well documented elsewhere. However, the station has an active History Club, which includes Service and ex-Service personnel from the local community who share an interest in these events and the units and people involved, and which has built up an extensive library of photographs that add additional flesh to the records. The club's involvement with the station goes back to before the Second World War and thus, with the benefit of personal recollection, it is able to produce this proud and lively record of day-to-day events at Manston over the years.

The study of history is not just an academic pastime recording events in chronological order. It is primarily about people and how their activities contributed to and made history. It also provides an insight into the lives of those who experienced the events. I consider that this book achieves this particularly well, and my gratitude goes to the Service and ex-Service personnel and those friends of Manston who have helped put it together. It is most fitting that those closely associated with the station should be the recorders of its history; after all it is they and their successors who have and will continue to make it.

Wing Commander David White

Introduction

The history of aviation in the Manston area is linked not only with the activities of the British air services, as illustrated in our successful first volume, *RAF Manston in Old Photographs*, but with early flying and pioneering activities as a whole at such venues as Eastchurch and Shellbeach on nearby Isle of Sheppey. The area's close proximity to the Continent has also contributed to it being the scene of interesting aviation events well before Manston became an airfield in 1916. To that end, attention has been given in this second volume of photographs to several organizations not noted in the first volume, or barely so, who none the less played their part at or in association with Manston. The compilers have taken a look back to pre-First World War days and included photographs of people and events which excited much interest locally as well as looking in more detail at RAF Manston. We are confident readers will appreciate this further selection of relevant photographs.

Although the 1920s saw the 'Geddes Axe' bring severe cutbacks to the services and swingeing restrictions were widespread, Manston continued to operate busily with a variety of units and aircraft in residence or merely visiting. The period was also marked by important and sometimes dramatic aviation events which touched the base. For example, when the giant airship, R.101, crashed in France en route to India on 5 October 1930, the bodies of those so tragically killed were given a guard of honour, provided by RAF Manston, on their return to Dover. The onset of 'Hitler's War' found the base prepared with anti-aircraft posts, camouflaged buildings and air-raid shelters. Control of Manston was vested in No. 11 Group of Fighter Command and much action by its aircraft ensued during the Luftwaffe attempts to subjugate the RAF fighter force in the Battle of Britain in 1940. The story of the airfield's part in this epic conflict has been often told and it is hoped that this book will pictorially complement the written accounts.

As the war progressed Manston became heavily involved in intense flying activities with virtually every type of aircraft using it either as an operational base or as a welcome refuge when lost or damaged in battle. A 3,000 yd runway, which still dominates the scene, was opened in 1944. Specifically designed to accept aircraft making crash-landings, it provided a veritable haven for many exhausted or wounded aircrew and their damaged machines. Subsequently this facility was enhanced by the introduction of FIDO, the petrol-burning system which dispersed fog and so permitted landings to be made in conditions of low or nil visibility.

The war years brought into prominence a number of services whose contributions to RAF operations and safety were most important and cannot be ignored. Radar is represented by the stations at Sandwich and Foreness. The former commenced operations in late 1943 as a fighter-control unit covering a wide area and with a range of about 100 miles. It was one of the largest, permanent Ground Controlled Interception (GCI) stations and with typical RAF humour was known in radar circles as a 'Happidrome' after a contemporary BBC comedy radio programme featuring a farcical music-hall. It closed many years ago and its place has been taken by RAF Ash, which is nearby. The Chain Home Low (CHL) station at Foreness was a trail-blazer in its fighter-control and raid-reporting roles, having operated from the earliest days of the Second World War. No trace of this historic site remains today.

The offshore raid-reporting of the RAF radar chain was complemented by the Royal Observer Corps (ROC) over the land. Staffed by 30,000 officers and observers (part and full time, male and female), the corps manned 1,400 posts in the 40 groups covering the UK. The fifty posts in Kent were undoubtedly kept at full stretch, day and night, throughout the war and none more so than those around Manston. On 24 August 1940 the extensive telephone network of the ROC proved invaluable to Manston when the bombing that continued throughout the day cut all communication with the airfield. Contact was only made possible by the gallant action of the Minster A1 Post's crew, Messrs E. Foad and P. Jezard.

The greatly increased air activity around the UK coastline during the Second World War highlighted the need for a safety service for airmen having to 'ditch' after combat. This was particularly necessary over the Channel and Thames Estuary. To meet this requirement the RAF Air/Sea Rescue (A/SR) branch was established with an eventual strength of 4,000 officers and men operating 300 launches. It is estimated that they saved no fewer than fourteen thousand lives before disbandment in April 1986. Ramsgate was the local centre for these operations which, in conjunction with A/SR aircraft, rendered vital life-saving aid to crashed or parachuted aircrew off the Kent coast.

Formed in March 1941, No. 438 (Thanet) Squadron, Air Training Corps (ATC) continues a close association with RAF Manston where its headquarters are located. Over the years the squadron has given preliminary military and aviation training to the boy and girl cadets who, whether they enter the RAF, another Service or remain in civilian life, will have benefited from their experience in the corps. On occasion, during the Second World War, the Thanet cadets' obligations and allegiance to the RAF took an unusually active form. On one occasion, they were called to the airfield to assist the servicing crews in the rearming, refuelling and making-up of ammunition belts. On another, on 12 February 1942, the lads worked on the fighters supporting the operation against the German battle-cruisers *Scharnhorst* and *Gneisnau*, and the cruiser *Prinz Eugen* escaping up the Channel. These and other chores they performed with great gusto. Almost fifty years later, in August 1990, the cadets were in annual summer camp at RAF Coltishall when the Iraquis invaded Kuwait. Their services were once again enlisted to help prepare the Jaguar aircraft destined for the Gulf War.

Following the end of hostilities the so-called 'Cold War' led to US Strategic Air Command (SAC) basing fighter bomber units at Manston, the first RAF station in the UK to be so used. A number of photographs in this selection were provided by American personnel of that period, some of whom are members of the RAF Manston History Club. Many hundreds of USAF officers and men served at the airfield between 1950 and 1958 and, despite the occasional rigours experienced, retain an affection for this corner of England which was their home for a brief time.

Shortly after the departure of the USAF the airfield became a 'joint-user', that is, it became available for both service and civilian use. Since that time there has been a continuous presence of airlines, flying-schools and maintenance firms, all located on the eastern side.

In 1961 'D' Flight No. 22 Squadron came on attachment and was quickly established as an integral part of local services with its Whirlwind search and rescue helicopters, which took part in many rescues of both service personnel and civilians. Despite strong local representations the unit was withdrawn in 1969 and Bristow Helicopters Ltd offered a civilian service. In 1974 the search and rescue unit returned in the form of 'D' Flight No. 72 Squadron and its Wessex machines, soon again to become 'E' Flight No. 22 Squadron. Finally, 1988 brought the Sea Kings of 'C' Flight No. 202 Squadron to continue the search and rescue role. The prospective loss of this much-prized local service in the near future is again causing concern. Other flying activities, related to the RAF and ATC, are those of the Air Experience Flight and the cadets' Gliding Club.

A resident organization housed in the main camp is the Defence Fire Services Central Training Establishment. The origins of air force fire-fighting and prevention go back to the First World War, when the immense growth of military flying necessitated the creation of a service dedicated to these tasks. From the early 1920s, at RAF Cranwell, the facilities have progressed from the Air Ministry Fire Service to the present-day Defence Fire Service. The training of staff similarly proceeded through such organizations as the Fire Fighting School (1922), the School of Fire Fighting and Anti-Gas (1943), the Fire and Rescue Training School (1959), up to the present Defence Fire Service's Central Training Establishment, set up in 1990. In addition to RAF firemen, civil, Royal Navy, airline, Commonwealth and foreign personnel are trained at Manston.

Such books as this and its predecessor rely wholly on material available and found by the compilers, and it is apparent that many aspects of Manston's intriguing past were not recorded photographically. However, we hope the reader will feel a reasonable and acceptable coverage has been achieved. Who knows, further photographs may yet be unearthed for a future publication.

1   PROSPECT PUB. HSE.
2   SITE OF R.N.A.S WESTGATE
3   BRITISH RAIL MARGATE
4   RAF MANSTON MAINCAMP
5   EXTENT OF ORIGINAL AIRFIELD
6   WAR FLIGHT NOW K.I.A.
7   PEGWELL HOVERPORT
8   SITE OF SUNKEN HANGAR

Earliest Beginnings:
Pre-First World War

The first airman to land an aircraft in Thanet arrived on Saturday 20 April 1912. Lt. Spenser D.A. Grey with his mechanic, Fred Brown, landed in a small field adjacent to St Lawrence College, Ramsgate. They had flown from Eastchurch on the Isle of Sheppey arriving in Thanet at about 6.45 a.m. Their aircraft, a Short Biplane Type S.34, powered by a 50 hp Gnome engine, after refuelling, took off from land adjoining Newby's brickfield.

A Short biplane at Westgate, possibly S.38. Beach House can be seen in the background. This area later became part of the RNAS seaplane base at Westgate. The S.38 saw much use at the Royal Naval Air Station, Eastchurch, and it was in this type of aircraft that Lt. Samson achieved the first take-off from a ship under way, the HMS *Hibernia*, off Weymouth, on 9 May 1912.

Opposite: Sqd. Cdr. Spenser D.A. Grey in the uniform of the RNAS, during the First World War. Grey was the first airman to land in Thanet on 20 April 1912. A pioneer aviator and one of the original and most experienced pilots in the RNAS, he learned to fly in the summer of 1911 at his own expense. Later appointed to the RNAS at Eastchurch, in September 1913 he flew Winston and Mrs Churchill and later gave the former flying lessons. At the outbreak of the First World War Grey carried out bombing raids from Belgium bases on Düsseldorf and Cologne and received the DSO.

With what looks to be one of Margate's major hotels in the background, a Short biplane, possibly S.34, attracts a crowd of visitors as she sits like a great bird awaiting her pilot, Lt. C.J. L'Estrange Malone, on 30 May 1912.

The Deperdussin Monoplane 'M.1' generates much interest at Quex Park, Birchington, after landing with engine trouble on 22 April 1912 during a flight from Eastchurch. The pilot on this occasion was Lt. A.M. Longmore, destined to become Air Chief Marshal Sir Arthur Longmore.

Piloted by Mr J.L. Travers and Mr Louis Noel, this Farman 'Waterplane' showed its capabilities by giving flying exhibitions and passenger flights at Margate in August 1912 as part of the *Daily Mail* Waterplane Tour. The photo-insert shows the tour's organizer, Claude Grahame-White, owner of Hendon and promoter of its aviation meetings in the years before the First World War.

Lt. Samson at Westgate, having landed his seaplane there after developing engine trouble mid-way between Dover and Sheerness, 13 May 1912. The aircraft was a Short Type S.41 powered by a 100 hp Gnome engine, and saw much service in both landplane and seaplane forms. It was later taken in tow by HMS *Recruit* and removed to Sheerness.

Short Type S.45 (RNAS No. T.5) visiting Margate on 30 May 1912 from its base at Eastchurch. By July of that year the aircraft had been fitted with floats, later reverting to a wheeled undercarriage for the army manœuvres of autumn 1912. The aircraft later saw service as a floatplane until struck off charge after it capsized in October 1912.

Another view of Short Biplane S.45 on 30 May 1912. Lt. Spenser Grey is inspecting the 70 hp Gnome engine while Lt. Sheppard makes his way to the rear of the aircraft. On the left, standing in front of Lt. Sheppard, is Lt. Malone and next to him the Mayor of Margate, Alderman Adutt. The aircraft was later flown back to Eastchurch.

Claude Grahame-White, organizer of the *Daily Mail*-sponsored Waterplane Tour, which took place in the summer of 1912. The aircraft visited Margate and were seen by thousands of visitors when at anchor off the Winter Gardens. The photograph captures the spirit of early flying and, clearly, no self-respecting pioneer would take off without the correct 'flying-clothing', including the neat bow-tie.

Mr Cecil Grace, pioneer aviator and the first instructor for the early RNAS pilots at Eastchurch, disappeared after leaving Calais while competing for the Baron de Forest Prize on 22 December 1912. Flying a Short S.27 powered by a 60 hp ENV engine, he was last heard passing over a Ramsgate fishing smack, the *San Toy*.

M. Manio arrived in his Bleriot monoplane in a field adjacent to George Hill Coastguard Station, Kingsgate, on Sunday 2 December 1912. He had flown over from Boulogne with his dog, Jim, who wisely decided to stay in Kingsgate when Manio took off only to crash later on to the roof of a house in Palmers Green, London.

Henri Salmet's aircraft, a Bleriot monoplane, on land lent by the local council at Cliftonville, Margate, in August 1913. In two hours Salmet took up nine passengers, the event being sponsored by the *Daily Mail*. It is perhaps no coincidence that the owner of the *Daily Mail*, Lord Northcliffe, lived nearby in Reading Street.

Salmet first arrived in Thanet on 13 August 1912 having flown from Gravesend. He was engaged by the *Daily Mail* to give displays nation-wide and in Thanet operated from a field, near the power-station at St Peters, which at that time formed part of Callis Grange Farm.

Ramsgate was chosen as the first control point for the *Daily Mail* £5,000 Round Britain Seaplane Race. The first competitor to arrive, Harry Hawker flying a Sopwith seaplane, landed outside the harbour on 16 August 1913. The then Mayor of Ramsgate, Alderman Gwyn, presented Hawker with a silver trophy at a ceremony held at the Pavilion.

Harry Hawker's Sopwith seaplane outside Ramsgate Harbour after landing to check in at the control point. This was the only aircraft of the original entrants to start the Circuit of Britain Race. Unfortunately Hawker had to retire through illness at Yarmouth.

A striking shot of a Short Pusher Seaplane (possibly S.79) powered by a 100 hp Gnome Monosoupape engine taking off from Ramsgate in early 1914. The old fish-dock forms the backdrop. Owned by Frank McClean, the aircraft was later taken into Government service but was completely wrecked in August 1915.

Short's 'Gun-Carrying' Seaplane S.81 (RNAS No. 126), powered by a 160 hp Gnome engine, at Ramsgate in August 1914 after being damaged by rough weather. The aircraft was later dismantled and returned by road to Sheerness. The S.81 carried a 1½ pdr Vickers quick-firing gun but was later fitted with an up-rated 6 pdr Davis Gun for trials on the Isle of Grain.

SECTION TWO
The First World War

In the years 1915 to 1918 the German naval airships' bombing campaign against England and especially the south-east was not without losses. The Zeppelin L.15 is shown wrecked off Margate after being hit by anti-aircraft gunfire near Purfleet on the night of 31 March 1916.

In an attempt to combat the German attacks, the Royal Flying Corps and the Royal Naval Air Service flew defensive patrols on receipt of warning of the approach of raiders. Operating from Manston, this BE2c aircraft of the latter service took part in many such sorties as a machine of the War Flight.

The transfer of the landplanes from Westgate to Manston in 1916 necessitated the construction of suitable hangarage at the new base. To meet this need an original Westgate hangar was removed and re-erected on the present Kent International Airport site. It was finally demolished in 1989.

The ex-Westgate hangar in the later years of its service at Manston in 1975. As well as other uses, it at one time housed the gliders of the Air Training Corps cadets. The design was a standard one, more widely seen on RFC aerodromes than those of the RNAS.

The original living-quarters for officers and men located in the East Camp or War Flight as it was called in the First World War, 1916. The road in the foreground, 'Coke Alley', was situated behind the hangars. The apparent patches on the roofs were a camouflage measure of the time. These huts were still extant in the 1950s.

Handley Page Type O/100 (No. 1456) was the second prototype of a line of very successful heavy bombers in the First World War. Arriving at Manston in July 1916 it joined the then forming Handley Page Squadron, with which it served until October 1917 mainly in a training role. On 1 August 1916 it flew – most unusually – a defensive sortie during a Zeppelin raid.

Officers of No. 3 Wing, RNAS, on arrival in France. The officers were mostly ex-Manston, where the unit was formed in 1916, its function being the bombing of industrial targets in the Saar. The CO, Wg. Cdr. W.L. Elder (left) is seated by Sqn. Cdr. R.B. Davies VC, and second from the left is Flt. Sub-Lt. R. Collishaw, destined to become a famous fighter pilot on the Western Front.

One of the Sopwith 1½ Strutter aircraft of No. 3 Wing in collision with a Ford car on the road which crosses the aerodrome. They manage things differently now and, with the aid of traffic lights, barriers and loud-hailers, keep airborne vehicles separated from those on the ground. In this case everyone had a laugh – except the insurance company.

Light-hearted RNAS officers, possibly pilots of the War Flight or No. 3 Wing, fooling about with the Manston steam-roller in the summer of 1916. Unfortunately the men are unidentified, though the officer on the extreme right looks remarkably like Flt. Lt. (at that time) Chris Draper, later called the 'Mad Major', famous for flying under bridges.

Souvenir from "Imperial Bazaar," Albion Hill, Ramsgate, which was twice wrecked by Zep. Bombs on May 17th, 1915, & June 17th, 1917.

On the night of 16/17 June 1917 two Zeppelin airships, L.42 and L.48, were en route to attack London when weather and engine trouble caused a change of target, L.42 bombing Ramsgate instead. The young lady is holding a souvenir of the raid, apparently a small bomb or similar object which fell from the airship.

Albert Street, Ramsgate, which suffered extensive damage as a result of the Zepplin raid at 0200 hours on 17 June 1917. Three people were killed, sixteen injured and damage was caused to the value of £28,159. A massive explosion shook the town following a direct hit on a naval ammunition store by a 600 lb bomb.

A Nieuport Type XI Scout calling in at Manston on 14 September 1916 and clearly arousing the curiosity of those present. Situated as it was in an area of much flying activity, Manston received its share of visiting aircraft from neighbouring aerodromes or those in transit and this was a typical example.

Sent to Manston in February 1917, this Hispano-Suiza-engined Sopwith Triplane joined the War Flight for evaluation under operational conditions. Although it flew a number of Home Defence sorties it was not put into production. This first prototype, N.509, was finally crashed on 29 October 1917 by Flt. Lt. A.F. Brandon.

The Manston War Flight flew a variety of aircraft between 1916 and 1918 but BE and Bristol Scout types predominated. This line-up of the latter was typical of the early 1917 period. N5392, first on the right, engaged in many Home Defence flights from April 1917 until March 1918 when it was crashed near Sandwich.

This Handley Page bomber (No. 3126) had a busy existence from its introduction into RNAS service in 1916 until February 1918 when it crashed in France after a bombing operation. The bizarre marking is associated with camouflage experiments in which it participated. The plane visited Manston briefly on three occasions.

An artist's impression of one of the ten twin-engined Gotha bombers which attacked Margate, Ramsgate and Dover from their bases near Ghent on 22 August 1917. As a result of the raid, twelve people were killed and twenty-seven injured. Three of the raiders were destroyed, this one brought down by local anti-aircraft gun batteries and crashing at Vincent's Farm.

One of the long-serving Bristol Scout aircraft of the War Flight, N5398 made a number of flights against the German raiders from January 1917 to August of that year when it was retired to a training role with the War School, where it was crashed on 16 August 1917.

Among its other chores Manston occasionally carried out service tests on new aircraft, such as this Armstrong Whitworth FK.10, numbered N511. Intended as a two-seater fighter its quadruplane wing layout was one of the unique designs of Dutchman Fredk. Koolhoven. It did not go into production.

This highly decorated Sopwith Camel (B3926) was probably the mount of an instructor of the Pilots Pool, Manston, in 1918. It had earlier served with the War Flight for a short time and later went to the flying school at Redcar. The starboard side fuselage carried the inscription 'Happy Hawkins'.

Avro 504C, No. 1485, was a training aircraft of the War School from May to the end of August 1917 when it was wrecked on landing by Flt. Lt. R.E. Darnton. This type of mishap was commonplace at flying schools, though usually without death or serious injury resulting.

In contrast to the previous incident, the pilot of this Sopwith Camel B5734 of the War School, 18-year-old Flt. Sub-Lt. W.N. Cross, was killed on 6 March 1918. Along with several other airmen who lost their lives at or near Manston, Cross is buried in Minster cemetery.

Ground crew members of No. 219 Squadron, Manston, with a DH.9 aircraft of the unit. Probably taken in late 1918 the photo shows the mixed nature of the personnel – ex-RFC and RNAS – to be found in all units of the RAF and who continued to wear the uniform of their original service.

DH.4, B9486, first saw service as an advanced training aircraft with the DH.4 School of the RNAS in January 1918. Subsequently it was flown by Nos 203 and 55 Training Depot Stations (TDS), the successive, large training units at Manston, until almost the end of the First World War. Although designed in early 1916 the DH.4 remained a high-performance aircraft.

A group of pupil pilots with their instructor during the course at No. 203 TDS, Manston, June 1918. The aircraft is a BE2c, a widely used training machine. From left to right: Mason, -?-, Stow, Fleischer, Scott, Moulson, Wickham (on the ground). Their uniforms confirm them as originally RFC cadets although they are now in the RAF.

Cadet Wickham ready for flight in a DH.6 of No. 203 TDS, Manston. Note the combined cockpit, the voice-tube for instructor/pupil communication, the gravity fuel tank below the upper wing and the brass, basic ignition switch. This elementary training machine was wryly known as 'The Clutching Hand' or 'The Dung Hunter'.

An early stage in the excavations in preparation for the first of the sunken hangars at Alland Grange in 1918. The spoil removed was deposited along the sides of the 'hole' and was largely chalk. The machinery used makes an interesting contrast with the equipment which would be utilized today.

Experiments to obtain early warning of the positions of raiding aircraft were carried out in the First World War using fixed or adjustable sound mirrors on the Kent coastline. Illustrated is the equipment of one such investigation on the Joss Bay cliff in 1918. Aircraft from Manston flew for some of the tests, which were only partially successful.

SECTION THREE

The Twenties and Thirties

Avro 504K, G–EAJQ, awaiting the first customers of the season, *c.* 1921. This particular aircraft, built in Manchester in 1919, attended the first Air Traffic Exhibition at Amsterdam in August of that year. Powered by a Clerget 130 hp engine the 504K was used extensively for pleasure trips during the 1920s and '30s.

The Avro 504K in military guise. E3798 was one of a batch of 500 built by Avro's during the First World War. This particular aircraft was used as a 'hack' or training machine by No. 9 Squadron when based at Manston in the early twenties.

Opposite: Capt. D. Milner Deighton at Margate in 1919. Deighton was an ex-instructor at the famous Gosport School of Special Flying where systematic flying training was first developed by Major R.R. Smith-Barry. The Avro 504 was used to give pleasure trips during the summer season and proved very popular with the visitors.

An excellent and detailed view of an Avro 504K with ground crew in attendance, during the early 1920s at Manston. Note the drip-tray placed under the aircraft to catch oil from the notoriously dirty rotary engine.

Airmen in their barrack room at Manston during the 1920s. It is interesting to note the old pattern uniform with its high dog-collar tunic fastened at the neck. The only heat within the barrack room came from a coke stove, which gives the impression that this particular photograph was taken in the depths of winter.

A postcard view of Manston dating from 1926. This particular card was posted to a Mrs Taylor of Sandwich and stated that the sender would be pleased to see her on the following Sunday. The view takes in most of the airfield, looking east along the road that cuts across the main grass.

Vickers Virginia J8239 of No. 9 Squadron after a crash-landing. The Virginia had been in collision with a Bristol F2B Fighter (J7666) of No. 2 Squadron over Manston on 14 March 1928. The two officers in the Bristol lost their lives. The pilot of the Virginia managed to crash-land in a field adjacent to the aerodrome.

'Armed to the teeth'. Vickers Virginia J6856 complete with 'fighting tops' in flight over Manston in 1927. As an experiment gunners' cockpits had been fitted in the top mainplane. Powered by 500 hp Napier Lion engines, J6856 saw service with No. 7 and No. 215 Squadrons before being struck off charge in 1937.

Vickers Virginia J8240 *Isle of Thanet* of No. 500 Squadron, based at Manston, 1931. On 4 June 1931 the aircraft was 'christened' with Kentish cider during a ceremony carried out by the then Mayor of Ramsgate, Alderman Terry. While serving with No. 7 Squadron the aircraft was badly damaged in a forced-landing at Sevenoaks but was later rebuilt as an Mk.IX.

Air and ground crew stand in front of Virginia J8240 'A' of No. 500 Squadron. The squadron, manned by half regular and half reserve personnel, suffered the fate of all Royal Auxiliary Air Force squadrons, being disbanded in March 1957. No. 500 Squadron had a strong connection with RAF Manston having been formed there as a Special Reserve Unit in March 1931.

An aerial view of Manston Main Camp, 1933. The aircraft in front of the hangar belong to No. 2 (Army Co-operation) Squadron. At that time the unit flew the Armstrong Whitworth Atlas, re-equipping with the Hawker Audax in May 1933.

Westland Wapiti IIa's of No. 608 Squadron visiting RAF Manston during the mid-1930s. The squadron was based at Thornaby and operated as a day-bomber unit of the Auxiliary Air Force.

Members of No. 2 (AC) Squadron in front of their Hawker Audax aircraft during their 1934 annual summer camp. That year saw them 'roughing it' at Friday Street, near Colchester, Essex. (The Army just had to get into the picture with their Vickers Tank.) No. 2 Squadron operated the Audax in the Army Co-operation role for nearly three years, finally re-equipping with the Hawker Hector. Today the squadron operates the multi-role Jaguar.

The carpenter's workshop in the mid-1930s, part of the School of Technical Training at RAF Manston. The syllabus within the school comprised a variety of trades and skills. All subjects taught led to a high degree of skill, needed to service the aircraft of the period.

Avro Prefect K5066 at RAF Manston while serving with the School of Air Navigation, later No. 48 Squadron. One of seven Prefects delivered in June and July 1935, K5066 was sold in May 1946 and operated on the civil market as G–AHVO.

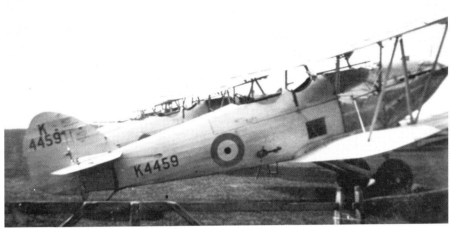

The family of Hawker biplanes are without question some of the most beautiful aircraft ever to grace the sky. Hawker Hart K4459 served with No. 500 Squadron at RAF Manston during the mid-1930s. This particular aircraft was part of a batch built by Armstrong Whitworth and delivered between January and May 1935.

A formation fly-past by Avro Ansons of the School of Air Navigation in 1937, during practice for the Empire Air Day. The photograph was taken from the top-turret of the leading machine. The Anson served with the RAF up until the early 1960s.

Avro Ansons of the School of Air Navigation in formation over Manston, *c.* 1936. The Anson was the first aircraft in RAF service with a retractable undercarriage. No. 48 Squadron, based at Manston, took delivery of the Anson Mk.I in March 1936.

The ubiquitous Avro 504N, J8761. This particular aircraft served with Nos 2 and 9 Squadrons and finally, in 1931, the Oxford University Air Squadron, thus spending its entire service life at RAF Manston.

A good air-to-air shot of Avro 504N, K2412, over Manston during the mid-1930s. It was one of two of the type serving with No. 500 Squadron during this period.

Personnel of No. 9 (Bomber) Squadron in front of one of the main hangars at Manston in 1924. The aircraft are, from left to right: Avro 504K, Vickers Vimy, Sopwith Snipe and a Bristol Fighter. The squadron was equipped with Vimys from April 1924 to June 1925.

Hitler's War

Minster Section, the Observer Corps, just after the outbreak of war in 1939. Later in the conflict uniforms were issued to the personnel (see p. 124). The Minster Section manned the posts adjacent to RAF Manston. Back row, left to right: Icke Horne, E. Chase (Landlord of The Bell, Minster), Bill Sackett, Ern Lucas, Jack White. Second row: Bill Petts, Norman Smith, Ted Young, Peter Young, Jack Player, Ted Foad, Percy Golder. Front row: -?-, Bill Slaughter.

Percy Golder of the Minster Section manning the post adjacent to the airfield. The device on the small plotting table is a Micklethwaite Height Correction Attachment, a very important piece of equipment which gave the height of enemy aircraft. The wall-chart was used for aircraft recognition, detailing both British and enemy machines.

The remains of No. 4 Gun Post after the Luftwaffe attack on 24 August 1940. This raid was one of the heaviest carried out by the Germans during the Battle of Britain period. Twenty enemy bombers attacked the airfield which brought a sharp response from the ground defences. Seven men died and the damage to the airfield was considerable.

A Light Anti-Aircraft gun, possibly a 20 mm cannon. Prior to the introduction of the 40 mm Bofors, the air defence of RAF Manston in 1940 rested with these light weapons. If anything, at least they could deter low-flying enemy aircraft. The 'erk' with his arm resting on the breach is Bill Brown. Perhaps the photograph was taken during 'stand-down' or a quiet period between raids. (An 'erk' was the general term used to denote all those unfortunates below the rank of corporal.)

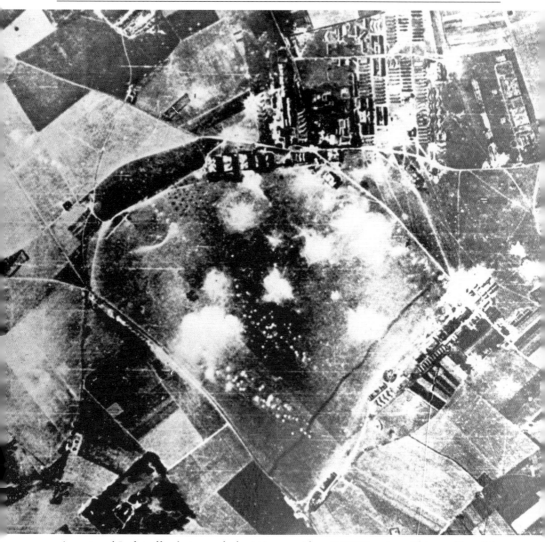

A captured Luftwaffe photograph depicting a raid on RAF Manston. This could well be the raid of 24 August 1940. The area was littered with craters and unexploded bombs. Communications had been cut leaving the station all but isolated.

Opposite: Fritz Buchner died when his Messerschmitt Bf 109E–1 crashed on Shuart's Marshes not far from St Nicholas at Wade on Monday 26 August 1940. Shot down by FO K.J. Marston of No. 56 Squadron, Buchner's body lay for many years buried deep in the Kentish clay. The wreckage and the young pilot's remains were excavated in 1984 and after a lengthy investigation Fritz Buchner was finally laid to rest in 1986, forty-six years after his last combat.

Spitfires of No. 92 Squadron take off from Manston in early February 1941. The squadron was one of the highest scoring units in the Battle of Britain. Their stay at Manston was fairly brief, being of only two months, and at the end of February they moved to Biggin Hill.

Members of No. 92 Squadron scramble. While serving at Manston the squadron was credited with shooting down the last Ju 87 (Stuka) to fall on British soil, on 5 February 1941. The Ju 87 had just attacked HM Trawler *Tourmaline* in mid-Channel. It was on the outskirts of the airfield that Plt. Off. R.H. Fokes of No. 92 Squadron shot down the German dive-bomber, which crashed at 9.50 a.m. killing its two-man crew.

A typical wartime Air Training Corps (ATC) cadet, George Bolton, aged 17, from Ramsgate. Note the old style tunic buttoned to the neck. Many young boys such as George later served with the Royal Air Force during the Second World War.

Fifty years on and past members of No. 438 (Thanet) Squadron ATC hold a memorial service on 21 April 1991 at Holy Trinity church, Northdown, Margate.

No. 438 (Thanet) Squadron (ATC) at Chatham House School, Ramsgate, 1942. During RAF operations from Manston, boys from the corps would help rearm and refuel aircraft, giving them a first-hand insight into life at a forward fighter station. A number of these young boys would later give their lives in the service of their country. No. 438 was formed in 1941.

Flt. Lt. Richard Playne Stevens DSO, DFC and Bar, a pre-war commercial pilot who became one of the first 'intruders' of note, operating from RAF Manston. Flying over Luftwaffe bases in France and Belgium he would attack any German aircraft or target of opportunity. He lost his life in December 1941 during a sortie to a German airfield in Holland.

Members of No. 174 'Mauritius' Squadron, Manston, 1942. Back row, left to right: Plt. Off. Hallett, Sgt. Seely, Sgt. James, Flt. Lt. McPhail, Flt. Lt. McConnel DFC, Plt. Off. Robinson. Front row, Flt. Sgt. Wettere, Flt. Sgt. Montgomery and Sgt. Tye. The squadron had been formed at Manston on 3 March 1942 from a nucleus of No. 607 Squadron.

Fleet Air Arm pilots from No. 841 Squadron leave their Albacore after a successful mission against enemy shipping. Lt. Walsh (left) and Sub-Lt. Patrick stand-down for a well-deserved rest at Manston, 1943.

Sub-Lt. Patrick and Lt. Walsh, preparing for yet another mission, confirm the target with the squadron's Intelligence Officer. No. 841 Squadron was finally disbanded at Manston on 1 December 1943.

Flt. Sgt. John Brooks of No. 174 Squadron in his Hurricane, Manston, March 1942. The squadron carried out fighter-bomber missions mainly against enemy shipping, later handing over their Hurricanes for the new Hawker Typhoons.

Members of No. 137 Squadron with their CO in front of their Westland Whirlwinds at RAF Manston in 1943. Powered by two Rolls-Royce Peregrine Mk.I engines, the Whirlwind proved a formidable ground-attack aircraft.

'R' Robert, Boston IIIa, of No. 88 Squadron, crossing the Channel in low-level formation with companions. On 22 October 1943 this aircraft returned from operations with its starboard engine burned out and landed at Manston having been escorted back by Typhoons of No. 3 Squadron, based at the airfield.

'R' Robert and pilot, Jack Peppiatt, who is the present co-chairman of RAF Manston History Club. The observer is Sid Kirk who was killed in Tunisia in 1943.

The grave of Flt. Lt. 'The Baron' Jean De Selys Longchamps DFC of No. 3 Squadron in Minster cemetery. The Baron, a second cousin of the King of Belgium and famous for his single-handed attack on the Gestapo HQ in Brussels, died while attempting a night landing in his Typhoon EJ950 on 15 August 1943.

An aerial view of RAF Sandwich Radar Station during the Second World War. One of the largest type GCIs in the Second World War, it came into operation in 1943 replacing both Willesborough (Kent) and Foulness (Essex). This type of Ground Control Interception station was facetiously known as a 'Happidrome'.

Hawker Typhoon R7752, personalized with the victory scoreboard of Sqn. Ldr. 'Bee' Beamont, of No. 609 'West Riding' Squadron operating from RAF Manston in mid-1943.

A group of WAAFs at RAF Manston, *c.* 1943. The WAAFs were the very backbone of the RAF and the maids of all work. The WAAF reached a wartime peak of 6,000 officers and 176,000 other ranks. Mrs Marjorie Everest, centre front, provided this photograph.

Members of No. 198 Squadron at Manston, January 1944. Among those present are: FO H. Freeman, FO J.F.H. Williams, FO Rainsforth, Flt. Sgt. J.S. Fraser-Petherbridge, WO J. Allan, Flt. Lt. J.W. Scrambler, Flt. Lt. D. Sweeting, WO H.A. Hallett, Flt. Lt. P.D. Roper, Flt. Lt. R.J. Dall, FO W. Parkes, WO G.J. Stokes, Flt. Lt. J. Niblett, FO W.G. Eagle, Flt. Sgt. R.C.A. Crouch, Sgt. J.S. Madgett, Flt. Lt. J.M. Plamondon, Flt. Lt. R.A. Lallemant.

Two WAAFs of the MT Section, RAF Manston, *c.* 1943. The Fordson tractor was the means of moving aircraft and the petrol bowsers round the airfield. The lady on the left is now Mrs Dorothy Daniel.

SECTION FIVE

Post-Second World War

Members of No. 77 Squadron at Manston in the summer of 1947 during Exercise Longstop. The squadron's role was to drop members of the Parachute Regiment on to pre-selected 'drop-zones'. The squadron was based at RAF Manston from September 1947 to November 1948. The unit took an active part in the Berlin Airlift, flying Dakota aircraft.

Air Marshal Sir Dermot A. Boyle KVCO, Air Officer Commanding Fighter Command, arrives at RAF Manston to carry out the annual AOC's inspection, 1955. He is being met by Grp. Capt. E.S. Finch, Sqn. Ldr. A. Lloyd DFC, Flt. Lt. J. Saunders RAFO and the Revd F. Gower Smith of Monkton.

A member of the famous Russian Bolshoi Ballet company is given a helping hand from one of the three TU 104s that landed on the airfield on 1 October 1956. The troupe of dancers later made their way to London by coach, the aircraft having been diverted to Manston because of inclement weather.

A view from the Silver City hangar with two Hermes airliners parked on the tarmac. The photograph dates from 1959: it was in that year that four Hermes were transferred to Manston. The site now adjoins the Kent International Airport complex.

Canberra WE168, a P.R.3 version of this famous jet-bomber, is edged into position after arrival from 231 OCU (Operational Conversation Unit). The aircraft served with Nos 540, 69 and 39 Squadrons, being struck off charge on 13 May 1969. The Canberra was a familiar sight at Manston but finally ended its days on the Fire Fighting School dump. The Spitfire stands on what is now part of the Spitfire and Hurricane Museum.

The Freedom of Sandwich is granted to RAF Sandwich on 3 July 1955. A detachment of WAAFs salute the Mayor of Sandwich outside the Guild Hall, giving a snappy 'eyes left' as they march through the old town.

The 'Luftwaffe' arrive at RAF Manston on Saturday 11 May 1968 to take part in the feature film *The Battle of Britain*. The aircraft flew in from Spain and close inspection reveals that the He111 bombers are in fact CASA 2.111s powered by Rolls-Royce Merlins. Wg. Cdr. 'Bob' Stanford Tuck was on hand to greet this unlikely armada, having had first-hand experience in attacking the real thing over Kent twenty-eight years earlier.

Members of the Italian 'Frecce Tricolori' in front of one of the team's Fiat G.91 jet-fighters during a visit to RAF Manston in September 1969. The Italians took Europe by storm with their high standard of 'display' flying, a standard the Red Arrows would later exhibit not only in Europe but throughout the world.

Visitors cast an 'expert eye' over one of the Manston Gliding School craft at one of RAF Manston's many open days. Young ATC cadets received their first taste of flying with the gliding school.

Air Vice-Marshal Clementi, with Wg. Cdr. Scott in attendance, takes a keen interest in the operation of the Air Traffic Control when visiting the Control Tower. The Air Vice-Marshal had been to the station on a previous occasion to present a Commendation to Cpl. McEvoy, who had been instrumental in setting up various sporting activities on the station.

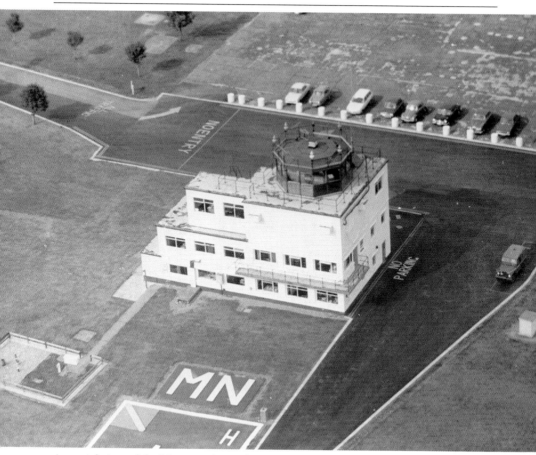

An aerial view of the Manston Control Tower, 1970s. The tower has seen many changes both externally and internally, although alterations to the building over the years have not changed the general shape of the structure. However, if one examines a present-day photograph closely, changes can be seen.

At first sight one would think this was a wartime photograph. Actually it was taken in the summer of 1973 when a visiting Hurricane dropped in. The personnel standing round the aircraft are, in fact, ATC lads casting an appreciative eye over this famous Second World War fighter.

A visiting Spitfire receives rapt attention from the youngsters during a flying visit in 1980. To add to the crowd's delight, the 'stunt stand-ins' from the feature film *The Empire Strikes Back* put in an appearance as well.

WD331, a De Havilland Chipmunk of No. 1 Air Experience Flight, at RAF Manston. The arrival of the first Chipmunk at Manston in 1968 enabled the local ATC cadets to gain 'powered-flight' experience. The first Chipmunk flew in 1946 having been designed in Canada. Powered by a Gipsy Major engine the aircraft has a top speed of 138 mph.

Flown by a member of the local air cadets, a glider from No. 617 Gliding School comes in to land at Manston. The school moved from Bovingdon to Manston in late 1970.

T.G. Aviation's hangar and clubhouse, which stand close to the eastern end of the runway. In 1983 Ted Girdler, a former Red Arrows pilot, set up his charter, aircraft hire and pilot training flying club. This family-run aviation business retains close links with the RAF presence at Manston.

THIS MEMORIAL
WAS ERECTED IN SEPTEMBER 1990
TO MARK THE FIFTIETH ANNIVERSARY OF
THE BATTLE OF BRITAIN
IN HONOUR OF
THOSE WHO DIED AND FOUGHT
FOR THEIR COUNTRY
AND TO COMMEMORATE
ALL THE PEOPLE OF THANET
WHO ENDURED THE CONFLICT

A simple memorial located outside the Spitfire and Hurricane Museum at Manston to mark the fiftieth anniversary of the Battle of Britain and to honour all those who fought and died for a freedom we take so much for granted today.

USAF at Manston

Manston, February 1952. Before the wooden barracks were constructed American Air Force personnel lived in tents. Canvas hung over a wooden frame with a wooden floor became a home from home for two years. Airman Bernard 'Shag' Shaughnessey stands in front of 'Tent City' on what is now part of the Spitfire and Hurricane Museum complex.

Manston's mobile snack-bar, December 1952. Hot coffee and doughnuts provided a welcome respite to those chill December winds cutting across the airfield.

The scene after an F–84 Thunderjet smashed into a field near Deal, Kent, following engine failure on 24 August 1952. Note the Coles Crane used to remove what remains of the aircraft.

Known as the 'Boxcar' or 'Packet', the Fairchild C–119 saw service not only in Europe but also Korea. Robust and ideally suited to operating from rough airstrips, these aircraft served the USAF for many years, ending their service in the early 1970s.

Early December and a Boeing calls to refuel. Occasionally aircraft such as this B-29 would drop in, which gave all those 1950s aviation buffs a real treat. In RAF service the B-29 was known as the 'Washington'.

'Life ain't easy, brother.' A fatigue party gets ready to clean and wax the floor in the Radio Repair Shop. Like all forms of service life, duties sometimes came down to what could be termed 'routine'.

An F–84 Thunderjet manufactured by the Republic Aviation Corporation wings its way across European skies. The variant in service with the 20th Fighter Bomber Wing, the F–84E, saw active service in Korea.

Sgt. Bayne of the 123rd Maintenance Squadron outside the Radio Repair Shop during the winter of 1952. Trying to keep warm through those cold English winters meant there was never a dull moment. The bucket of coke and the shovel tell their own story.

Looking into the shark's mouth – the air-intake of an F–86, May 1953. The F–86 'Sabre' first flew in 1947 as a single-seat fighter-bomber. The 406th Fighter Bomber Group based at Manston were re-equipped with the F–86F and the unit was redesignated the 406th Fighter Interceptor Squadron.

USAF personnel 'putting their backs into it', making their own 'sidewalk', 1953. A late September sun makes the task less arduous. These 'guys' will no doubt be looking forward to an evening at The Crown or Good Intent, two of Margate's pubs with warm welcomes.

The hangar on the right, which is still extant, was used by the 514th Fighter Bomber Squadron, that on the left by the Maintenance Squadron and the low, central building was that unit's Orderly Room. This housed the Squadron Commander's and other offices in which the paperwork was handled and personnel records were kept.

Another 'Alert' during August 1953. With helmets, side-arms and carbine these two NCOs are just about ready for anything. One thing you could say about serving at Manston is that life was never dull.

'This is me, Mother.' The boys outside their beloved tent. Back row, left to right: Thompson, Easley, Kaehlen, Merriell, Wilson. Front row: Haare, Kent, -?-. According to the caption on the back of this photograph, 'we all lived in this tent from 1951 to 1953'.

An F–86 single-seat interceptor, 113509, sits on the hard standing at Manston in August 1953. This particular aircraft served with the 514th Fighter Bomber Squadron and was fated to crash on 3 December 1953 killing its pilot, Capt. Burrows.

The 406th Air Police Squadron on parade, Manston, 1955. It is interesting to note that a detachment of USAF Military Police was also based at Ramsgate and Margate civil police stations (to keep wayward airman on the straight and narrow, no doubt).

T/Sgt. Malcotte and M/Sgt. Vannekovan with the 514th Fighter Interceptor Squadron mascot, 'Russell' the goat, Manston, 1955. One wonders what became of Russell – retirement on a local farm perhaps?

The crew-chief makes one last check before take-off. The aircraft is a T–33 manufactured by Lockheed. These aircraft were based at Manston to train pilots in the fighter-bomber role.

Entering into the yule-tide spirit, Santa grabs a ride in an A/SR helicopter. It is Christmas 1955 and Flt. Lt. G. Rideout (on the left) and Sqn. Ldr. P.A. Alt (with his young son) provide an escort for dear old Santa. It should be remembered that the American service men at Manston spent a lot of time and effort making life a little bit brighter for some of the less well-off youngsters in Thanet.

Grp. Capt. Gordon Oldbury, the Commanding Officer of RAF Manston, inspects the station, December 1955. USAF personnel man the Control Tower and carry on with their air traffic control duties. The young officer on the extreme left of the photograph looks as if Christmas could not come soon enough.

The Orderly Room personnel together with the crane crew, Manston, 1955. The 'Lorain' could lift loads in the region of 6 to 8 tons. One has to ask how they all got down again.

A view of the Control Tower during the mid-1950s. As on all airfields the tower is the focal point of all air movements. Compare its appearance with that of fifteen years later (p. 82).

An informal shot of Col. Manson (left), officer commanding USAF personnel at Manston, and Grp. Capt. Oldbury (centre), commanding the station, December 1955.

The final parade as the American personnel march towards their barracks for the last time on 30 June 1958. Eight years service came to an end as the various units and squadrons were distributed to other bases both within the UK and in Europe.

An F–84 Thunderjet rests outside the 512th Fighter Bomber Squadron hangar at Manston, *c.* 1957–8. The 512th together with the 513th and 514th, all part of the 406th Fighter Bomber Group, were assigned to 3rd Air Force. This hangar, located on the Loop, still exists at the western end of the airfield.

The slogan on the sign outside the 512th Fighter Bomber Squadron hangar says it all – 'Pride Of The 406th F.B. Grp. Envy Of The 513th and 514th F.B. Sq. Justification For The 406th'. The photograph was taken in mid-1958 and it would not be long before all this unit's pride was but a memory as Manston said farewell to the USAF later that year. To some it was the end of an era. . . .

SECTION SEVEN

Lifeline Manston

An Albion vehicle in use as an ambulance at Manston, *c.* 1937. Having first been used in 1914, Albion vehicles were for a long time associated with the British air services. One model for the RAF, the Type AM.463 chassis, proved to be particularly versatile and saw use as fire-engines, petrol bowsers, general-purpose tenders and mobile dental surgeries as well as ambulances.

With the large-scale use of float planes and flying-boats by the RNAS and RAF in the First World War a need for motor-boat tenders arose, their function being to assist in handling these aircraft when water-borne or to give aid when circumstances caused forced landings at sea. RAF.959 was one of those in use at Westgate in 1918.

ML.123, an armed motor-launch designed for RN use, against the harbour wall at Ramsgate, where it was based, in 1918. Larger and faster than RAF seaplane tenders, it could operate in liaison with Westgate's machines in more distant offshore areas due to its superior seagoing qualities.

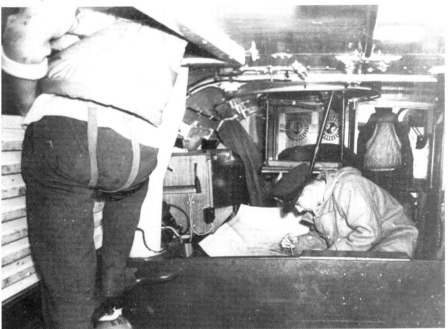

The small amount of space below, all that was permitted by the 63 ft length and 17 ft beam of the standard Air/Sea Rescue launch, was reminiscent of a submarine. Looking forward, the navigator is seen at work in the 'chartroom' with the circular mounting of a gun-turret beyond and above. It was said that 'Whaleback' rides were better recalled than remembered!

Originally crews of Second World War Air/Sea Rescue boats preferred not to carry armament as life-saving was their concern. However, two launches were sunk by German attacks in August 1941 so machine-gun turrets were then fitted. Three more boats and twenty crew were lost at Dieppe in August 1942 and thereafter 20 mm Oerliken cannons were carried.

Personnel of the Air/Sea Rescue service based at Ramsgate Harbour, c. 1943. The launches normally carried a nine-man crew comprising the skipper (a commissioned officer), first- and second-class coxswains, two deckhands, two engineers, a W/T operator and a medical orderly. Clothing was an assortment of oilskins, sou'westers, roll-neck pullovers, flak-jackets and Mae Wests.

A USAF Flying Fortress crew which had 'ditched' are picked up safely. Launch 189 from Ramsgate was called on to retrieve these flyers who, apparently, had quite efficiently carried out their 'ditching drill' by launching the Fortress's own inflatable dinghies and boarding them. They are about to join No. 189.

A/SR launch 149, Ramsgate, pulls alongside a relieved Plt. Off. Reynolds on 20 May 1942. He had bailed out 18 miles east of South Foreland but carried out the 'drill' in exemplary fashion – got rid of his parachute, inflated his dinghy and Mae West and erected his radio mast complete with flag. A perfect pick-up.

The increasingly aggressive actions of the enemy air and sea forces towards the A/SR launches resulted in the introduction of heavier armament. Twin Lewis machine-guns were fitted at the stern plus a single Lewis in each turret. At a later date Browning guns replaced the Lewis and an Oerliken cannon was added.

No. 127, with its turrets and Oerliken cannon, was typical of the more heavily armed 'Whaleback' class of A/SR launch. This boat served at Calshot, Dover and Ramsgate in the period June 1941 to May 1946 until damaged in a collision. Here it is departing from Ramsgate at low tide.

The most commonly used Air/Sea Rescue launches were the 'Whaleback' and 'Hants and Dorset' classes, No. 149 being one of the sixty-five of the former type. This boat had a long period of service from August 1941 to May 1957.

In spite of much local opposition the SAR helicopter coverage by the detached Flight of No. 22 Squadron at Manston was withdrawn in March 1969. After more than two years its place was taken by the civilian Bristow Helicopters Ltd who began their contract in June 1971. Illustrated is one of their two silver and orange coloured Whirlwind machines operated on behalf of HM Coastguard until the return of the RAF in October 1974.

Two Westland Wessex HAR.2 helicopters of 'E' Flight, No. 22 Squadron, display themselves before the Manston Control Tower in the late 1970s. The Wessex, powered by two Bristol Siddeley Gnome engines, saw much use in the search and rescue role around the UK in the hands of Flights of Nos 22 and 72 Squadrons.

Manston's first RAF search and rescue unit was 'D' Flight of No. 22 Squadron which commenced operations in July 1961, flying Westland Whirlwind HAR.10 helicopters. These machines were fitted with Alvis Leonides Major piston-engines and were eight- to ten-seater general-purpose machines built to the basic design of the Sikorsky S–55 type.

During their stay at Manston, from 1950 to 1958, the USAF provided search and rescue facilities in the form of 'A' Flight of the 9th Air Rescue Squadron and the 66th Air Rescue Squadron at different periods. Both were equipped with these Grumman SA-16 Albatross amphibians and had access to the B-29 Superfortress adapted for long-range searches.

Opposite: Manston's Commanding Officer, Wg. Cdr. D.B. Wills DFC (left), presenting the citation of the Air Force Medal to Flt. Sgt. Ian Jones (from Birchington) in March 1968. The award resulted from gallant action by Jones in the previous September when a Whirlwind of No. 22 Squadron rendered aid to a German yawl in distress. Flt. Lts Laycock and Burningham look on.

A Sikorsky S–55 helicopter of the 66th Air Rescue Squadron being demonstrated to an admiring crowd in the 1950s, apparently at an open day at Manston. The USAF units were the first to operate helicopters in the search and rescue service in east Kent from their Manston base.

An impressive view of a Westland Wessex HC.2 at its Manston dispersal when serving with 'E' Flight of No. 22 Squadron in the late 1970s. XV730 was not built, originally, for search and rescue duties but was converted to that role. Note the squadron badge on the fin, incorporating the Greek letter 'P', symbol for Pi and adopted by the squadron in 1915.

An inspection of the FIDO (Fog Intensive Dispersal Operation) installation by a party of senior RAF officers in 1957. Fifteen UK airfields were fitted with this system of lifting fog above a runway by heat, generated when vapourized petrol was burned from a line of pipes running along both sides of the main runway.

Installations of the FIDO varied, with some having pipes above ground level, others having them recessed in channels, as at Manston. Becoming operational here in April 1945, it was the last FIDO in use and having safely landed more than 120 aircraft was closed down about 1959. Electronic landing aids had made the system obsolete.

The 'foam carpet' was introduced at Manston in 1964. This was a system which enabled aircraft with undercarriage damage or malfunction to land with wheels up without risk of fire as a foam carpet was pumped on to the runway smothering any sparks generated by the friction. This Canberra from Cottesmore successfully landed with the aid of foam on 30 April 1969.

A sheet of foam spray marks the passage of a Handley Page Victor 'V' bomber down the runway as it makes an emergency landing, caused by undercarriage trouble, at Manston, 8 January 1968. The large parachute has been deployed to provide braking during the aircraft's slide on its belly. Quite a number of Victor and other 'V' bombers were 'customers' of the foam landing system.

With a satisfactory conclusion (a controlled crash!) reached in this incident, the Victor sits on the runway surrounded by the usual airfield emergency vehicles while preparations are made for its removal. Worthy of note is how straight – despite the circumstances – the pilot has managed to keep the aircraft: not always achievable.

One of the four aircraft making use of the foam carpet in 1977 was this Blackburn Buccaneer. In its sixteen and a half years of operation the system assisted forty-four military and eighteen civilian machines to make safe landings. The types ranged in size from the Beagle Basset to various 'V' bombers and a DH Comet airliner.

An Avro 748 of Skyways, one of the many civil aircraft to make use of the foam carpet, lands without injury to the crew or twenty-six passengers on 9 May 1968. A maximum area of 3,600 × 90 ft, using 100,000 gallons of foam and costing £3,500, could be laid. A combination of technical and economic factors caused the system's withdrawal in October 1980.

Members of the Manston Fire Service undergoing routine practice in the 1970s. Those present are Messrs D. Duff, D. Sutter and A. Harris. The service was staffed by civilian firemen employed by the RAF. The uniform, it will be noted, differs considerably from that in use today.

A unique view of the crash/fire station in the 1970s. The photo is especially interesting as it shows all the services prepared for an actual emergency landing on the foam carpet. Both civilian (right) and RAF ambulances (left) are present with the fire-engines poised at the threshold of the building.

A bulk fuel tanker of the 1950s at Manston carrying, as the marking specifies, AVTAG (also known as JP–4), the aviation fuel with an additive. By this time high-pressure refuelling had superseded the Second World War bowsers and tanker capacities were in the 1,000 to 3,500 gallon range with a delivery rate of 500 gallons per minute.

The entrance and guard-room to the Second World War radar station at Sandwich. Relinquished by the RAF many years ago the site is now the scene of various commercial activities. The station was part of the UK radar chain for approximately fifteen years and played a major role in our air defence of south-east England from 1943 to 1945.

The Main Operations block as it appeared in 1993. This was a brick and concrete blockhouse opened in 1943. It swept to a range of 100 miles, between approximately 3,000 and 60,000 ft, and had an establishment of about 160 RAF and WAAF personnel. Various aerial arrays were located in the adjacent fields. In case of emergency a stand-by site existed at Sholden.

SECTION EIGHT

Miscellany

Thanet Aviation Ltd., Ramsgate

PRESENT A

GRAND FLYING DISPLAY

AT THE FLYING GROUND,

Nethercourt, Ramsgate

on SUNDAY, JULY 17th, 1932

From 2.30 till Dusk.

First Personal Appearance in Thanet of

Miss AMY JOHNSON and Mr. J. A. MOLLISON

DEMONSTRATION FLIGHTS BY THE 'AUTOGIRO.
AEROBATICS BY MR. D. H. STACE (the famous Aerobatic
Pilot of Capt. Barnard's 1931 Circus).
"ELOPEMENT TO GRETNA GREEN"
An Aerial Comic Interlude featuring
GEORGE THOMAS and the Ramsgate Entertainers.
PARACHUTE DESCENT BY MR. A. W. FAIRLIE
The World-renowned Parachutist.
BOMBING THE CAR.   AERIAL SHARPSHOOTING.
Passenger Flights All Day from 5/-
Admission 1/-. Children 6d. Car Park: Motors 1/-, Motor Cycles 6d.
Teas and Refreshments can be obtained on the Ground.

The 'Grand Flying Display' promoters of the 1920s and '30s were nomadic, numerous and very busy during the summer months of those years. This is a typical local press advertisement of the time and on this occasion the added attraction for potential Thanet customers was the presence of the two famous long-distance flyers, Amy Johnson and Jim Mollison.

Early flying days at what became Ramsgate Airport. The four-passenger DH.83 Fox Moth carries the colour scheme of Hillman Airways Ltd who commenced a Romford–Ramsgate service in June 1932. Three aircraft of this type superseded the similar number of Puss Moths which were originally employed.

The grave of Lt. Cdr. Eugene Esmonde VC, DSO in the Gillingham, Kent, cemetery. He was killed in heroic circumstances on 12 February 1942 when leading six Swordfish aircraft of No. 825 Squadron of the Fleet Air Arm, taking off from Manston. Their task was a torpedo attack on the German battle-cruisers *Scharnhorst* and *Gneisenau* and the cruiser *Prinz Eugen*.

For many years, apart from the First World War period, postcard views of areas and subjects of interest found a ready market both locally and with visitors. So far as security regulations permitted, RAF stations were quite often featured by commercial photographers. In this 1926 print the attractions of both village and camp are combined.

Occasional visitors to Manston were Bristol Britannias from No. 99 or No. 511 Squadrons of RAF Air Support Command. The aircraft shown is XM518. Entering service in 1959 the type could carry approximately 140 passengers and was fitted with four Bristol Proteus engines. Britannias were also widely used by civilian airlines.

Another aircraft to make fleeting appearances at Manston was the long-range, maritime-reconnaissance Avro Shackleton, in service in this role from 1951 to 1962. In addition to patrols of long duration round UK shores from bases in Northern Ireland and south-west England, Shackletons operated out of Gibraltar and Malta. One of the type remained airborne for 24 hours and 21 minutes.

A Vickers Valiant high-speed, high-altitude bomber of the V-Force visits Manston on an air-day. The Valiant saw eventful service from 1955 to 1965, participating in the Suez campaign, dropping Britain's first atom and hydrogen bombs, forming part of NATO air forces and making a significant contribution to the development of refuelling in flight.

Air shows, displays or extravaganzas held at RAF Manston in past years have invariably included an exhibition by the Falcons, the RAF's own display parachutists. In recent years they have jumped from aircraft supplied by the RAF but on 12 October 1971 the Army's Red Devils descended from this civilian DH Rapide.

Personnel of the Minster ROC in 1942 (Royal Observer Corps since April 1941). Back row, left to right: F. Golder, J. Smith, E. Lewis, E. Spanton, P. Golder. Second row: J. White, R. Hammond, F. Winter, E. Chase, N. Smith. Front row: W. Petts, E. Butcher, P. Jezard, D. Bewden. Their A1 Post, in the background, was located on the A253 road abreast the main runway.

This Gloster Javelin, XH764, was on display from July 1967, for some years, at Manston. It was a high-performance, two-seater, all-weather fighter of the period from 1955 to 1967, during which it served with eighteen squadrons of the RAF in the UK and overseas. It was powered by two Armstrong Siddeley Sapphire engines and its production ran to 430 aircraft.

No	SURNAME	NAMES	AGE	ADDRESS	TOWN	DESCRIPTION	ADMITTED 1940	DISCHARGED	TRANSFERRED	1940
1054	OUSLEY	Gladys	16	15, Alexandra Road	Ramsgate	A	cas	24. Aug	24. Aug	PRESTON HALL	AIR RAID
1055	LUCAS	Alfred	69	82, Boundary Road	Ramsgate	A	cas	24. Aug	24. Aug	-do	AIR RAID
1056	HILL	Alfred	27	1103933 A.C.2. S.H.Q.	R.A.F.	B	cas	24. Aug	24 Aug	-do	
1057	STEAD	William	85	36, Park Road	Ramsgate	A	cas	24. Aug	25 .Aug	-do	AIR RAID
1058	THOMPSON	Charles	21	36014.29/Pte 'C' Coy	6th Bn BORDER Regt	B	cas	24. Aug	24. Aug	-do	
1059	BROOKER	James	23	2062695 Gnr. 342 Coy	R.E.	B	cas	24 Aug	25 Aug	UNIT	
1060	DEBENHAM	Kenneth	20	PILOT OFFICER 151, Squadron	R.A.F.	B	cas	24. Aug	26. Aug	HALTON	
1061	HUNTLEY	Donald	38	A.F.S. A.R.P.	Ramsgate	A	cas	24. Aug	25. Aug	HOME	AIR RAID
1402	COOK	Frederick	45	103, Winstanley cres	Ramsgate	A	cas	25. Aug		HOME	AIR RAID
1403	DEBLING	William	43	13, Montefiore Cottages	Ramsgate	A	cas	25. Aug		HOME	AIR RAID
1404	MEDHURST	Mabel	18	17, Station Approach Rd	Ramsgate	A	cas	25. Aug		HOME	AIR RAID
1405	ALLEN	Ernest	56	50, Chilton Lane	Ramsgate	A	cas	25. Aug		HOME	AIR RAID
1406	PHILPOT	Rose	47	65, Winstanley cres	Ramsgate	A	cas	25. Aug		HOME	AIR RAID
1408	JOHNSTONE	.A	43	3902162 /Pte	521 COAST BATTERY	B	cas	25. Aug		UNIT	
1085	RAWLINGS	James	40	D33415 Pte H.D.	6th Bn. BUFFS	B	sick	25. Aug		UNIT	
1064	SAYER	William	72	24, Woodford Ave.	Ramsgate	A	cas	26. Aug	27 Aug	UNIT PRESTON HALL	AIR RAID
1065	EFFMERT	Willi	24	29/51596 FELDWEBEL	GERMAN AIR FORCE	B	cas	26. Aug	30. Aug	ROYAL HERBERT HOSPITAL WOOLWICH R.A.F. HOSPITAL	ESSMERT GERMAN 7/4.45.
1066	WALKER	William	27	PILOT OFFICER 616, Squadron	R.A.F.	B	cas	26. Aug	27. Aug	HALTON	
412	GOLDFINCH	Thomas	60	8, Victoria Road	Ramsgate	A	cas	26. Aug		HOME	AIR RAID
416	YOUNG	Ronald	19	909550 A.C.1. FLIGHT, S.H.Q.	R.A.F. 12 SERVICING	B	cas	27. Aug	27. Aug	MANSTON	
418	SKINNER	Alfred	23	4619905 Pte. ANTI-TANK Coy	198th INFANTRY BRIGADE 8th (IRISH)	B	sick	27. Aug		UNIT	
421	DOBSON	Joseph	23	Pte.	8n. KINGS H.M.O. DULCHOEILA	B	sick	27. Aug		UNIT R.N.	
1090	GARNER	Victor	21	SEAMAN R.N. PATROL	90- FERVENT	B	cas	27. Aug		SICK BAY	
1091	COOK	Raymond	21	28, Station App. Road	Ramsgate	A	cas	27. Aug		HOME	AIR RAID
142	LURCOOK	George	19	110, Hereson Road	Ramsgate	A	cas	27. Aug		HOME	AIR RAID
143	CHANDLER	William	48	43, Napleton Road	Ramsgate	A	cas	27. Aug.		HOME	

An extract from the Ramsgate Hospital register covering the period from 24 to 27 August 1940. Except for three, all were 'casualties' as opposed to 'sick' cases and included Army, Navy, RAF (pilots and ground crew) and civilian personnel together with one German airman. Note the predominance of cases due to the air raids at that time. The name of the German (from the crew of a destroyed Dornier bomber) was Essmert and not Effmert as incorrectly recorded.

Two former adversaries meet at Manston. In the cockpit of Manston's Spitfire, TB752, sits Adolf Galland, former commander of II/JG26 during the Battle of Britain. In 1940 Reichsmarschall Göring asked Galland what help he could give him to defeat the RAF. Galland's famous reply was, 'a Staffel of Spitfires Herr Reichsmarschall'. Galland visited Manston in 1983 and had to make do with a single Spitfire, not a 'Staffel'.

The station commander, Wg. Cdr. Tom Hindmarsh BA (centre), welcoming a number of his predecessors at the time of Manston's 70th anniversary as an airfield in 1986. The group are standing in front of Station Headquarters. Unfortunately it has not been possible to identify them for this publication.

Acknowledgements

This second publication has been compiled and written by the following members of RAF Manston History Club, all aviation enthusiasts with a particular interest in Manston's past as an RAF base: Frank Cheesman, Douglas Cockle, Roy Doherty, Jack Peppiatt and John T. Williams.

The Club would like to express its thanks to past and present Commanding Officers for their support since the club was founded in 1986: Grp. Capt. Tom Hindmarsh OBE, BA (retd), Wg. Cdr. Jim Whitston, Wg. Cdr. Alastair Montgomery MBE, MA and Wg. Cdr. David White.

The following are offered our sincere thanks; if we have missed anyone out we apologize unreservedly:

Eric Appleton • The H.A. Buss Collection • Dan Clark • H.A. Clayfield
Ken Cox • Nigel Douglas • Mrs M. Everest • D. Golder • Ron Hammond
Isle of Thanet Gazette • The F.J. Keble Collection • Tony Moor
RAF Manston History Club • The R.P. Ross Collection • Norman Smith
No. 438 (Thanet) Squadron ATC • Geoff Williams • Walt Wilson.

Aircraft illustrations by Jack Peppiatt.